Praises for the

Max's disabilities have not stopped him from having a happy life. Max is a great brother and is much loved by me, his niece Jodie, nephew Craig, brother in-law John and all his family.

I am very proud of him and what he has achieved in his life. This book is a testament to that.

From loving sister, Kaye Anderson

Max has a great attitude to life that allows him to get the most out of each and every day.

He does not complain he just gets on with it. He is admired by his friends and carers and much loved by his family.

Max often says his life completely changed when he moved into his unit in Brookvale where he was able to begin to live independently. For the first time he had his own space which has enhanced his life so much.

I am very proud of him and hope his efforts in writing his story results in it being told as I am sure it will be inspirational to many others living with disabilities.

Helene Johnson (sister)

My brother, Max is a well liked person and everyone you talk to says what a well-mannered and polite person he is. Very sports minded, he is a one-eyed supporter of the Penrith Panthers Rugby League Football Club. He also loves cricket and watching the Olympic Games.

His love for travelling brought him to the Whitsunday Islands, South Australia, Canberra and Western Australia three times. Shortly he is heading to Brisbane.

He received his own unit from Department of House fourteen years ago and he has not let his disability stop him in anyway. He is a wonderful brother.

Ken Stone

THE BENEFIT OF THE DOUBT

Living With Cerebral Palsy

Written by

Rodney Maxwell Stone

BALBOA
PRESS

A DIVISION OF HAY HOUSE

stonerodney@bigpond.com

Balboa Press books may be ordered through booksellers or by contacting:

Balboa Press
A Division of Hay House
1663 Liberty Drive
Bloomington, IN 47403
www.balboapress.com.au
1-(877) 407-4847

ISBN: 978-1-4525-0565-7 (sc)
ISBN: 978-1-4525-0566-4 (e)

Because of the dynamic nature of the Internet, any web addresses or links contained in this book may have changed since publication and may no longer be valid. The views expressed in this work are solely those of the author and do not necessarily reflect the views of the publisher, and the publisher hereby disclaims any responsibility for them.

The author of this book does not dispense medical advice or prescribe the use of any technique as a form of treatment for physical, emotional, or medical problems without the advice of a physician, either directly or indirectly. The intent of the author is only to offer information of a general nature to help you in your quest for emotional and spiritual well-being. In the event you use any of the information in this book for yourself, which is your constitutional right, the author and the publisher assume no responsibility for your actions.

Printed in the United States of America

Balboa Press rev. date: 06/16/2014

FOREWORD

When Max Stone asked me to write the foreword to his life story, I was both surprised and honoured.

I first met Max in August 1992, when I started the DEB course. I took an instant liking to him because of his quick wit and his ability to make quick comebacks and humorous comments when you are talking to him.

When I read his book, I discovered that we have a few things in common. In the book, Max tells some funny stories about falling over and getting himself into some embarrassing situations. He has knocked himself unconscious. I'm always falling over too, but unlike Max, I have never knocked myself out. The most damage I've ever done is to have broken my nose.

Max also relates the difficulties he has when he goes out into the community. Having a speech problem, it's often hard for Max to make himself understood. People sometimes don't take the time to listen, or they assume that he is intellectually disabled. I can identify with this situation, as I, too, have a speech impediment.

I enjoyed Max's book very much. It is extremely entertaining and informative, especially as it is written from a disabled person's perspective. Max describes the difficulties he has faced with nursing homes, including both the costs involved and the conditions. He also discusses issues like public transport and sheltered employment.

I hope that many people will read and enjoy this book as I have. I also hope that, when they read it, people will learn that all disabled are not the same, and not automatically assume that we all have intellectual disabilities.

Yours sincerely,

Janette Carey

INTRODUCTION

My childhood was different from that of most other children. I went to a special school that offered more individual attention both in the classroom and in therapy sessions. My first teacher used her imagination and creativity to design pieces of equipment to replace the pencil so I could do my schoolwork.

Leaving school and starting work meant I had to live away from home. There weren't suitable sheltered employment opportunities for me, or those places that were close by didn't want to know me because of my limited hand functions. In my opinion, this situation made a joke of the term "sheltered workshop."

Working away from home has meant staying in a nursing home with elderly people because of a shortage of proper hostel accommodations. This story documents the experiences I have had living in these places.

Although, it was through living in a nursing home that I met a very good friend. We enjoyed each other's friendship for eighteen years before he died. Overlapping that friendship was a renewed relationship with my twin brother.

There are a couple of reasons why I have written my autobiography. Firstly, I wanted some sort of record of my life so far. I have reached that objective to my satisfaction. Secondly, I wanted to provide insight into the good times and the bad times during the life of a person with a disability.

Thank you for reading this introduction. I hope you will go on to read and enjoy my story.

I chose to republish my manuscript because the first time it wasn't quite up to standard. Now I can present something of which I'm proud.

Rodney Maxwell Stone (Max)

Sometime before, during, or immediately after my birth, something happened to cause my twin brother, Kenny, to enter the world more physically able than I. Mum and Dad realised there was something wrong with me when I was about six months old.

This meant I had to travel from Mildura in Victoria to Penrith, which is just west of Sydney. Uncle Colin had the task of bringing me to Grandma's place. Needless to say, I don't remember anything about the trip, not even the spoon that Colin said I had a hold of and wouldn't give back to the staff aboard the train. Grandma then took me from doctor to doctor to see if they could tell what the problem was.

By the time I was four, my family had settled in Penrith, which is where Mum had grown up. Our house was just a street away from Grandma and Grandpa's place. Those were the days when I had to be looked after by someone because domestic economic conditions forced both Mum and Dad to work. Although Grandma, Great-Grandma, aunties, and such helped, this responsibility rested primarily with my sister, Helene. She was only seventeen months older than me. She reluctantly gave up valuable playing time to perform this duty. When Kenny and I were older, the chore went to him as well as Helene.

As in most children's lives, the big day came to start school, although I was about three years older than would be considered normal. On the first morning the taxi called for Mum and me to take the journey from Penrith to Parramatta. This was the unusual mode of school transport I took for five years, morning and afternoon. The trip was nineteen miles. Mum and Dad contributed ten shillings a week, as was the price in those days.

When we arrived at Northcott School for Crippled Children, we were met by my teacher, Miss Brabam, who was an elderly person, and another lady, Mrs Rigby, who was a nurse's aide. She was there for those children who needed help with eating their lunch or going to the toilet. I said a tearful goodbye to Mum, although Miss Brabam told her to just go and not say anything. The learning process had begun. Initially I was placed in a class that was termed "The Slow Learners' Group," probably because of my age and my limited use of my hands. In a classroom that was half a day learning and half a day playing, and through my teacher, who was also the officer in charge of the school, I obtained a solid basis for an education.

Amid constant interruptions, Miss Brabam did wonders with her teaching. Because I couldn't use a pencil, she employed an old printing set, spending hours mounting words on strips of cardboard for me to arrange into sentences. She also wrote short stories on large sheets of cardboard, leaving out key words. I had to place the correct word in the space provided. There was a box that Miss Brabam designed. It was divided into twenty-six compartments. Each hole had a number of small cardboard squares. On each square was a letter of the alphabet. I had to make words or sentences out of them. Often, the pieces of cardboard were scattered from the effect of my hands spasms. Miss Brabam more or less guessed whether the schoolwork was correct. I can't recall how arithmetic was done, except I remember trying to write big numbers on large sheets of paper using a hand splint to hold the pencil.

Two or three years went by, after which Miss Brabam decided to retire. This upset me greatly, though I really don't know why. It was a tough period, and I was often seen crying without any apparent reason. They found me crying at home and not wanting to go to school, where I cried almost daily, making the excuse that there wasn't anyone to have a game with. That really wasn't the problem because I had always been a loner out in the playground. This was very strange behaviour, considering I hadn't had any real liking for Miss Brabam. Our new teacher, Mrs Grice, was very nice. I would have been at the age of eleven or twelve. After six weeks or so of driving everyone mad, I returned to virtual normality.

Just after I started school, Mum and Dad found out about the Spastic Centre of New South Wales at Mosman. This was an organisation specialising in the care and treatment of spastic children. The doctors there said that I had cerebral palsy. After making their diagnosis, they recommended that a pair of short irons would help me with walking. I probably didn't wear the irons correctly because many times I could hear Mum or Dad call out, "Max, stand up straight and walk properly."

Falling over was part of life when I was growing up. Nearly every day I would tumble to the ground, sometimes escaping any injury, other times taking skin off somewhere on my body. The first really bad fall I had was at Northcott. One afternoon, when I was waiting for the taxi, I had hold of a railing. The next thing I knew, I was regaining consciousness in the front seat of the taxi. I had fallen down the steps of the school entrance.

The doctors also suggested some things to Dad that could be made to improve my standard of life at home, one of which was a table where I could eat my meals. It was lower than the normal kitchen table with a semicircle cut out of the front so I could sit right in and not fall off the chair. Dad put a dallying peg on the right-hand side of the table to hang on to while I tried to feed myself. My parents argued about how much help I needed to eat my meals.

Growing up in Penrith with Helene, Kenny, younger sister Kaye, and of course, Mum and Dad, was mostly a happy time. The other kids sometimes involved me in their play, and other times I was just an onlooker. Sometimes I trailed after them over to the park across the road from our place to play on the swings, merry-go-round, and slippery dip. This was one of the places other kids gathered from all around the neighbourhood. They could always tell I was different from them by the way I walked. They often asked, "What's wrong with your brother?"

Mum and Dad gave me a chain-driven three-wheeler bike for my ninth birthday after I fell in love with the one at school. The bike was my link to the outside world, and I rode it everywhere. Apart from riding the bike up and down the driveway and everywhere else around the house, I ventured out onto the footpath that ran past our front gate. We lived in the middle of the block, so this meant I could go either way. I enjoyed going in the left-hand direction, where the pathway was smooth. I had to dodge the people walking to and from the shops or work, many of whom I came to know. If I went to the right, the ride was much tougher.

Beyond our next-door neighbours' house was a petroleum storage depot. Its driveway outside the boundary fence was badly broken up, and some of the slabs of concrete in the footpath had sunk down. This made my bike-riding dangerous. When I first got the bike, fear had me staying away from this section of the path. Then, when I became braver (or sillier), my riding skills were tested. Other than the couple of times I fell off and skinned myself, I could generally ride over this rugged journey without much trouble. The bike came in handy when we went visiting. I was able to ride down to Grandma's house or around to Aunty Mary's. Helene often took me on it to Grandpa's barber shop for a haircut.

As a small boy I spent a lot of time playing alone. Other than riding the bike, toys didn't hold much of my interest. While other kids built cubby-houses, billycarts, or whatever, I created in my mind. It wasn't unusual for me to go around for days or weeks thinking about something that I would have liked to make or construct.

At times I felt frustrated that my ideas couldn't be put into reality. One of my mental creations was a building shaped like a cross. It had one room at the bottom, three rooms in the middle and another room at the top. Each room measured six feet square (in the old measurements), and it was built from fibro and iron bars. I also planned to build it from—of all things— corrugated sheets of plastic and bush sticks.

Another contraption that I would have liked to make was a steam engine— perhaps not a big steam train but merely an engine mounted on a tabletop that I could somehow fire up. This idea came from a small working model I once saw. There must have been a thousand other things that ran through my mind.

When I was young, I also spent many hours pretending to be with someone. I could be found seemingly talking to myself when there wasn't anyone else around.

Other than the few sad times, much of my childhood was filled with uncontrollable laughter; when someone told me or did something funny, I would laugh longer than normal. Sometimes I thought of the joke hours later and that would start me laughing. People would ask me, "Why are you laughing, Max?" Often, I wouldn't tell them. This giggling would often start at mealtime, which made an otherwise leisurely meal disruptive, or I may have had a laughing fit when the occasion called for seriousness, at times making a fool of myself. I always knew what was happening but couldn't do much about it.

At school it was the practice to have a period of occupational therapy, physiotherapy, or speech therapy. My session in occupational therapy was five mornings a week, beginning at a quarter past nine. The purpose of this therapy was to use and improve my hand functions. Some of the activities were putting wooden blocks with holes on a peg board, doing up large buttons that were sewn on pieces of material attached to blocks of wood, and learning how to catch a large felt ball. Sometimes we went outdoors to have a game of cricket or French cricket or to kick a ball around. At one stage we grew our own flower garden.

Once, the therapists had a "self-help week," during which they tried to find out how much we could do for ourselves. Other than plugging electric cords into power points, opening and closing doors and drawers or the like, we were asked to take off and put back on a jumper. I don't know why, but I became embarrassed when it was my turn to take the jumper off, and I refused. This was strange behaviour, considering I was about ten. A couple of days later, when shyness wasn't such a problem and I had seen other kids removing their pullovers, I showed them how to do it.

When I was heading into my teenage years, there were two or three people that I liked very much and put high on a pedestal. They were young women, and all, strangely enough, were my occupational therapists. I suppose I thought I was "in love" with them. Perhaps I should point out that these ladies didn't all work at Northcott at the same time. Considering that they were ten or twelve years older than I was, this feeling of immense admiration must have been unnatural.

It became so bad at one stage that I asked Kaye to write a letter to tell one of the ladies how I felt. The idea was to drop it into her handbag. I sat through the occupational therapy session with this note clutched in my right hand and, amazingly, was not asked what it was. I don't know what I would have done if I had been questioned about it. After the session I went across the corridor and flushed the small piece of folded paper down the toilet.

One day a salesman came to the school selling electric typewriters, which were state-of-the-art in those days. The school decided to buy three of these typewriters for pupils like me to use to do our schoolwork.

Learning to use the electric typewriter became part of my occupational therapy. I tried several ways of typing. Eventually, and quite by accident, we found a way I could strike the keys accurately, with my right arm placed on the desk in front of me and my left arm resting on the other. This seemed to steady my movement, which gave me enough control to tap one key at a time using my middle finger. I still use this method some forty years later.

Having mastered the electric typewriter (somewhat), I was able to move on to more conventional education. From The Slow Learners' Group I went into second grade, having to do the last term before going onto primary school. It felt strange because suddenly I was with kids three or four years younger than I.

When I entered this new form of education—or new to me—I began to do subjects that I'd never heard of. During the first week our teacher, Mrs Myer, asked me, "How do you think you'll go with dictation on Friday?" I asked myself, "What do they mean by dictation?" After the class spent the whole week learning to spell a list of words, by Friday it had all fallen into place.

There were two main problems I had as that school term went on. After a couple of weeks, something went wrong with my new typewriter, and it took a few weeks to be fixed. When the typewriter was finally repaired, I found that keeping up with the class on dictation day was impossible. When the time came to type what the teacher read out, I would become nervous and tense. This problem stayed with me long into third grade until the half-yearly exams, when the teacher, Miss Howell, went to my typewriter to mark the dictation. She found very little typed on the paper.

In February 1960 Mum and Dad decided to lease the new Mobil Service Station in Penrith, or Mobilgas, as it was known then. This meant Dad was giving up his job as a Civilian worker at the army camp, and Mum resigned from her position at Woolworth's. Both of them were employed in Penrith, so they were well-known and well-liked. This was one of the reasons why the business turned out to be the success it eventually was. Dad arranged for the taxi to drop me off at the garage every afternoon after school. As a family we gathered to eat our evening meal, although over the years, as the family grew up, our gatherings at the garage became more infrequent. My bike was there, and I rode it all over the driveway, except the main part of the drive, where the vehicles came in. I stood for hours watching the men grease cars and do the mechanical repairs.

One of the more unfortunate things about having my parents in business was that I felt that I, if not all of us, lost our father in some ways. Being a service station proprietor took up almost sixteen hours, seven days a week. For instance, Dad used to put my boots and leg irons on before he went to work, but once he had to open the garage so early, there wasn't time for him to do it.

I went away from home for the first time at twelve years of age to a hostel called Beverley Park, which was in Campbelltown, southwest of Penrith. The hostel was a home for physically handicapped boys. They boarded there during the year and attended a school that was also on the large property. At year's end some of the boys went back to their homes. This made space for other lads who wanted a break from their families (or vice versa). In my case, it was Mum needing some respite from me.

The first couple of evenings I was at Beverly Park, I cried from home sickness. I remember a nurse saying, "You'll be here just long enough to get used to the place. You'll not want to go home." That was exactly what happened. At the end of the four weeks, I was walking around telling people, "I don't want to leave here."

I found company playing with the boys, many of whom were around my age, and a couple of them I knew from Northcott.

I spent several happy periods at Beverly Park. It was a life that suited me. I even became accustomed to going early to bed, which was midafternoon. They would bathe everyone and put them to bed, and then let us occupy ourselves by watching television or playing games.

One memory I have of Beverly Park is that I had some really bad falls. The first morning after I arrived the night before, we were all sitting down for breakfast, and the next thing I knew I was lying on my bed. The fall on my head had rendered me unconscious. The next year, again on the first morning, I didn't even reach the dining room. I made it just to the foot of my bed when I slipped on the highly polished floor. Once again I was sent into a state of unconsciousness. A condition was put on my next stay, which was that I should wear a crash helmet when walking.

At around this time, I was heading into my teenage years and, as for anyone, this period was vital. The problem was that no one explained what was happening. I maintain to this day and will do so forever that, if someone had taken a moment or two to tell me all about life at the appropriate time, adolescence would have been much happier. It was also around about this time that I had a tendency to throw a tantrum or two. One evening, Helene, Kaye, and I were in the kitchen. We had just finished tea, and they asked me to carry my empty plate to the sink. I wouldn't do it and kept arguing that I would drop it. Finally, in a mad rage I slammed my fist down, breaking one of Mum's good dinner plates.

We were all fighting one night, and something happened that made me run into the bedroom in a temper, slamming the door behind me. The next thing I knew, they opened the door to tell me I had knocked Helene out when I slammed the door. When I looked out, I could see her lying on the lounge, but her eyes were open.

I saw Kenny go through his adolescent years. This was the era when young men dressed up to go out. That meant he received or brought suits, sport suits, white shirts, ties, and fancy shoes. He would go to the pictures at night with friends or a girlfriend while I was left sitting on the lounge in my pyjamas. I think I was about sixteen before I wore a sports suit. Even then it was a hand-me-down from Kenny.

Kenny left school and started work early in life. This allowed him to buy his first car at the age of about fifteen. It was an old F J Holden that badly needed restoring. I think the plan was to have the car roadworthy before he was given a driver's license.

One evening when I was at home alone and feeling bored, I went outside, walked to the F J, got in the driver's side, and pretended to drive. The feeling of having a steering wheel in my hands must have overwhelmed me. I looked down to see the key in the ignition, turned the key, and pressed the starter button. To my surprise, the engine started. I tried to turn it off, but the key had fallen out. I began to panic. A thought ran through my mind that, if I blocked off the exhaust pipe, the motor would stop. I jumped out of the car and found a piece of rag. I held it over the end of the exhaust pipe and hoped the motor would stall. While I was still trying that, Kenny walked up the driveway and saw the bother I had got myself in. Kenny hurried over to the car and picked up the key, which had fallen on the floor. He tried to put it back into the ignition but couldn't, so he used some sort of light. I forget just what it was—maybe a cigarette lighter. We discovered that the keyhole was on a half turn, which explained why the key didn't go back in. It is stating the obvious to say I would have liked to learn how to drive, but in reality I didn't have the physical capability to hold a driver's license.

Sometime during my early teenage years, Dad came home with the news that the Spastic Centre had opened a factory for employing people with cerebral palsy after they left school. Dad thought I might be interested in applying there for a job.

While it all sounded very good, I was still in something like the first year of high school, and felt I would like to further my education. I remember saying, "I don't wanna be a dope." My interest became stronger after our school went on an excursion, so we decided it would be something for the future.

That was in 1961, and by this time there were two taxis taking about ten students from Penrith to Parramatta. Each cab would pick up from either side of the old Great Western Highway; that is, they collected kids from houses just off the highway.

It was in fifth class when we heard the news that the Crippled Children's Society was going to open a new school at Kingswood, just outside Penrith. I became excited at the prospect of not having to travel so far to school every day.

Our new school began in a hall owned by the Church of England. The morning the school opened, I arrived in the taxi to be greeted by the mayor of Penrith, Mr. Chapman, and a couple of members from the local newspaper, *Penrith Press*. They took a photo of Mr. Chapman and me shaking hands to put to the story that was run. This article was the first of some much-needed publicity to make people aware of the existence of children with disabilities and to help raise money for the new school building.

At the entrance to the old church hall were three or four steps, which meant that anyone who was in a wheelchair had to go around the back, where there was a ramp. When we went inside, it all looked quite barren, with its bare floorboards and no ceiling. At the other end of the hall stood a stage that was used for the church's performances. We used it for our school productions, too. On either side of the stage was a doorway. One doorway led to a small kitchen and the other to a room that was used for our various therapies.

Our first teacher at the new school was Mrs Bruner, who was a very nice lady, but at the same time quite strict. It took a while for her to settle into the new job, although she had worked with us for a short period back at Northcott. After two or three months, during which the classes were disruptive and unorganised, I said to Mum, "I wish I could go back to the old school. This is too unorganised." When it all settled down, we made up for lost time. Mrs Bruner really piled on the schoolwork.

Although I had enjoyed my friendships at Northcott, there were three schoolmates with whom I developed a very strong bond at Kingswood. One of these mates was Norma, who started school a few months after me. She had a physical condition that affected her from the waist down, and she walked with the aid of two metal sticks. As the years went by, she was eventually confined to a wheelchair. When Norma first began travelling in the taxi with us, her mother really had to fight to get her into the car. There was a crying episode every morning for a while. After a while things got better. When Norma's shyness subsided, she started to talk to the cab driver, although we didn't have the same one every day. The strange thing was that, when Tony, who was much older than we were and who sat in the front seat, boarded the taxi, Norma would retreat from her standing position behind the front seat to sit in the corner on the back seat.

In the early days Norma and I didn't share the same classroom but were often seen in the playground together. From about second grade on, we were put in the same group and always enjoyed each other's company.

Throughout the ten years that Norma and I went to school together, I don't think there was a cross word between us. Norma was happy to lend a hand anywhere she could. When my hands couldn't perform a task, she was right there helping. She would act as an interpreter when someone couldn't quite understand what I was saying.

Gary also began at Northcott just after I did at age seven. He had the misfortune of swallowing a dummy when he was six months old, which left him with cerebral palsy. Gary walked with a full-length calliper on each leg and crutches to add support. He wore a leather-padded hat to protect his head when he fell. Gary also had poor eyesight, which made the learning process that much more difficult for him.

The second electric typewriter went to Gary because he had limited hand functions. He used the thumb on his left hand to press the keys. Unlike me, he didn't seem to have any spasm—that is to say, he was always in control of his arm movements.

While we were still at Northcott, it was decided to take Gary, Peter, and me away from the main dining room because we needed extra assistance to eat our lunch. I mention this only because this is where I came to know Gary well. Gary was a lively lad, a real chatterbox. People always knew he was around by the constant talking. In fact, I think he drew people to him by the chatter, his wit, and his personality. Gary would often say, "I love talkin'."

One of Gary's and my favourite pastimes was to discuss the latest recordings on the top forty that we heard on the radio. The conversation would go something like this: "Gary, have you heard the new song by the Easybeats?" I would ask.

Gary would reply, "You mean 'Friday on My Mind'? What a good record. Have you heard that one by the Hollies, Max? I think it's called 'Bus Stop.'"

I'd reply, "I must buy that one. Do you like 'Good Vibrations' by the Beach Boys?"

Gary would answer, "It's not bad." Then Gary might turn around from his position, which always seemed to be in front of me in the classroom, and say, "I love 'You're My World.'"

I would say, "I'll buy that one, too," and on it went.

Another hobby of Gary's was playing the mouth organ, holding it in his paw-like hands. He played by ear, and he could hear something on the radio and then perform it. I think Gary would be the first to admit he was no Larry Adler, but it brought many hours of enjoyment to him and his friends alike.

Gary loved test cricket and spent hours listening to it on the radio. One day we were out in the playground at the church hall, which didn't have a fence. A stranger pulled his car up under a shady tree and began to eat lunch. I don't know how Gary knew this man was listening to the cricket, but being as outgoing as he was, Gary walked up to the car and started talking to him. There isn't much doubt in my mind that Gary was really inquiring about the cricket score and not trying to strike up a new friendship. It was because Gary and I talked so much that he could help other people, like Norma, understand my speech. People would often say, "Listen, Gary, can you tell me what Max is saying?"

Bruce was the third person whose friendship I valued. He was quite able-bodied except he suffered with asthma, which affected his schoolwork. It was thought that he might do better at a school like ours. I really can't recall when Bruce started at Northcott, although we shared the same taxi. It was amazing how he adapted to children who had various afflictions. The first day that Bruce started, I heard his mother say to the cab driver words like, "Bruce is going to help wherever he can," and help he did. Nothing was too much trouble for Bruce. He pushed people along in their wheelchairs, picked things up when we were unable to bend down, and generally helped pupils and staff. There was so much done for me by Norma, Gary, and Bruce that I feel sure that a simple "thank you" was never enough.

It must have been the end of 1963 when Mrs Burner decided to leave us. She was replaced by Mr. Hilton, someone we also knew as a teacher at Northcott. He also spent three weeks with us earlier that year while Mrs Bruner was on leave. As time went on, I found Mr. Hilton to be tremendously understanding. He realised perfectly my physical limitations, sometimes even making excuses for me that weren't really warranted. He was the same with the other pupils, always wanting to help people to do their best. One example of this was with a boy at school called Alan who was a quadriplegic. Alan put in hard work to represent Australia at the 1964 Paralympics in Tokyo. Mr. Hilton made a special point to introduce Alan to every visitor who came to our school. I really don't know if this paid off financially or in any other way, but it showed how much Mr. Hilton thought about his students.

When there was more than one teacher at a school, they shared the playground duties. Mr. Hilton was seen playing some sort of sport with us every day.

We loved to play cricket, and Mr. Hilton would help Gary to support him while they each had a grip on the handle of the bat. Hours were spent hitting fours and sixes all over the playground.

Early in 1965 work commenced on our new school building, which was just up the road from the church hall. Being so close, we were able from time to time to stroll up and see how the building was progressing. Sometimes we got in the way of the builders, but generally they were very good because they cleared a path for us.

After six to eight months the school was finished, and we could move in. I recall the first day we changed locations. With the new school came a new set of rules. For instance, we had to use one door to enter the building and another door to go out. There was a strange rule about the younger boys using the girls' toilet. Gary and I decided to try out the new emergency system, which was a call bell similar to that in hospitals. I made a five-dollar bet with Gary that he wouldn't be game enough to flick the switch and activate the alarm. To my surprise, Gary jumped out of his chair and leaned towards the switch, which was close to his desk. The next thing we knew, bells were ringing all through the school. One of our attendants, Mrs Jeffrey, came rushing into the classroom to see what the trouble was.

Later that day, when Mrs Jeffrey and Mr. Hilton were in the classroom with all of us, Mrs Jeffrey "dobbed" on us, though I don't know why. She said words like, "I heard bells ringing this morning." After that we were lectured on just what the emergency system was for. When it was all over I turned to Gary and said, "Double or nothin'."

The new playground was still being laid with turf, which meant that the playing area was restricted. Most of our playing was done under a sheltered area. This was fine until Fred fell and broke an arm running around one of the brick poles that held the roof up. After this accident two things happened.

A wooden fence was built between the two brick poles to stop people from running between them, and we had a table tennis set assembled to occupy us while the playground was being established. Table tennis soon became the favoured sport, even over cricket, at school.

When we moved into the new school, a strange thing happened to me. I found it difficult to concentrate on my lessons. In those days, when we reached high school, a correspondence course was introduced, and we had a package of lessons called a set sent to us from the correspondence school. The idea was to complete a set of work each week. In the beginning I could keep up with the workload and was quite proud of myself for doing so. As time went on and schoolwork increased, I found it wasn't possible to keep the pace.

In 1966 Helene married David, and I turned eighteen. Thoughts of leaving school went through my mind that I mentioned to Mum and Dad, and they seemed agreeable. All there was left for me to do was decide what I wanted to do for the rest of my life. I had two or three options. One was to stay at home and amuse myself. This wouldn't have been such a problem. As I've indicated before, I love music and had a substantial collection of records that would have kept me entertained. I also didn't mind watching television. Another option was to try to obtain a job at Centre Industries, which would mean living away from home. I really wanted to get away from home and make a life of my own. It would give me a social life living in a hostel with people around about my age. The third alternative was to work in a sheltered workshop, of which there were several scattered around Sydney.

I had to inform Mr. Hilton of my decision. I went to school on a Monday morning and asked Mr. Hilton if I could have a word with him. We went to his office, and I explained the situation. Mr. Hilton agreed with our decision. He offered me the services of a social worker from Crippled Children's Society to plan my future. Six or eight months went by, during which I was interviewed by social workers to help me to decide where to work and live. Of course, my first choice was Centre Industries but this wasn't possible because of the lack of room in their hostel. Eventually we decided on the sheltered workshop at the headquarters of The Crippled Children's Society in Sydney. This meant living away from home. It was suggested I should be close to work. I had never heard of nursing homes and didn't have any idea what they were. The only time I had anything to do with nursing was at Beverly Park, a hostel where I stayed during some Christmas school holidays. I chose to try the workshop and nursing home arrangement.

The last day of school came. It unfolded with Mr. Hilton's asking me to write a letter to my correspondence schoolteacher. I don't think I ever did. All the excitement must have gotten the best of me. The lunchtime bell rang, and everyone headed to the dining room—everyone except Mr. Hilton and me. He kept me talking while everyone was settled. When Mr. Hilton received some sort of signal, we walked to the dining room. We entered to find a surprise party being thrown for me (although it was somewhat spoilt when Mr. Hilton and I mistakenly walked in on the preparation earlier). The day ended with everyone standing around the taxi saying a sad goodbye.

Other than a couple of occasions when I was invited back to the school for functions, I lost contact with my three friends. The times that I saw them, it didn't seem quite the same. Mr. Hilton, whom I didn't see after the day I left school, went to teach in Fiji. Gary went on to be very successful in the field of greyhound racing. The last I heard, Bruce was going to marry Norma.

Two days after I left school, it was time to move into the nursing home. I had mixed emotions about it all. On one hand, I felt happy to be leaving home and meeting new people. On the other, I didn't know what I was letting myself in for as far as the nursing home was concerned.

We arrived at Willandra Nursing Home in Marrickville on a Sunday afternoon. The building looked fairly new and had about fifteen steps leading up to the front entrance. After climbing the steps, we were welcomed by the sister in charge, Sister Middleton, who took my particulars from Mum. Then we were shown my room, which I was to share with an elderly chap named Mr. Dawson.

After a restless night, my first work day came. A station wagon from the Crippled Children's Society came to pick me up. There were a few other people aboard whom the driver had picked up along the way. When we arrived at the workshop at Redfern, I was taken in and introduced to some of the management and staff.

I was given a job with a man named Warren, who also had cerebral palsy. The job entailed quality control of battery tops. These were four-inch squares of Masonite in which two springs were inserted. On the reverse side was a strip of cardboard covered with foil and held on by a staple. We sat at a table, and our job was to sort through the redboard, as it was called, piece by piece to check if it was assembled correctly.

The first day's work finished, the trip back to the nursing home began. For some reason we took a different way home. Instead of being first or near first to be dropped off I was the last, arriving home about six o'clock. This situation improved a couple of months later when we started to catch taxis and arrived home around four thirty in the afternoon.

When I arrived home that first night, I was greeted by young Nurse Smith, who assisted me with the evening meal and a shower. Later that night, Dr Cook came to visit me, as it was mandatory for anyone in a nursing home to have a doctor.

A young man at Willandra, Peter, had been involved in some sort of accident. As time went by, we were joined by two other men, Ted, who was blind, and Noel, who had the misfortune of catching encephalitis. All of us attended the sheltered workshop.

I don't know how many times we changed rooms. As I said, I started off by sharing a room with Mr. Dawson. Then Ted moved in, and it was decided to put Ted, Peter, and me in a room together. After Ted and Peter had an argument, the matron thought it would be better to separate them. Ted and I shared a room for a while. When Noal moved in, we found ourselves in a five-bed ward just inside the front entrance to the nursing home.

Spent fifteen months in the nursing home and workshop environment, during which there wasn't much social life for me. I went to a social club where we worked occasionally but didn't fit in well with the crowd.

One Saturday afternoon in October 1967, Mum came to see me. She had heard that I hadn't been well. This was a slight illness that kept recurring. Mum said to me, "I think you better come home." She went on to say that, because Kenny had just married, "I haven't got a boy at home now." I willingly agreed to go home. When I look back on those days, I see that they were a complete waste of time and money. There wasn't anything gained by it.

The next seven years were spent living at home without any daily outside activity. There was a sheltered workshop that commenced operation quite close by. We went for an interview, but they didn't seem to be interested in taking anyone with a handicap like mine. There was a trial period suggested, but we didn't hear any more from them. This made annoyed me. It had me asking myself, "Why have a sheltered workshop if they aren't going to employ people who are in most need of it?"

Within that seven-year period Kenny and Wendy were blessed with Dwayne and Nicole. Kaye and John married and had Jodie and Craig, and Helen and David also had Bradley and Kylie. I was able to feel an uncle's love for each nephew and niece, and this brought me many hours of enjoyment.

In 1968 Mum and Dad bought and moved into a brand-new home at South Penrith. This gave me some interest, as we slowly moved our belongings into the house. We also had the lawn and garden to establish. I like to think that my hands were lent to this task. (Well, I did move the hose a few times.) My days were filled with listening to the radio, watching television, and playing records.

The taste that I have in music was then and still is very liberal. My record collection had about 345 records, along with many albums of all kinds of music, ranging from classical to the latest pop music. It may well be said that listening to my records turned me on—that is, when I was listening to them, it was difficult for me to sit still. I found myself rising to my feet, pretending to sing to a make-believe audience. Music filled a large part of my life. The one thing I would like to do in my life is to sing or at least to play a musical instrument.

Perhaps it's unfortunate, but I didn't read much in those days. Reading has always been a slow, uncomfortable process for me. In fact, I wouldn't be surprised to learn that I have dyslexia to some degree. I don't mind flicking through a newspaper or magazine. Mum once said to me, "It's a shame you don't read, Max. It would occupy a lot of your time."

In February 1969 I received a letter from the Spastic Centre asking if I would like to do an assessment period at Centre Industries for nine days, living in the hostel and working in the factory. I was thrilled with the opportunity.

I really enjoyed this term and trying several different jobs. One job I had to do was putting what seemed like plastic washers on shiny chrome bolts. This was done using a jig, which is a mechanical device designed to hold a component in place during machining.

The toolmakers at Centre Industries had become renowned for how they adapted everything from large machinery to small bits of equipment, spending many hours developing a way one particular person with cerebral palsy could operate a lathe, a drill, or another type of machinery. Sadly, at the end of that trial period, I had to return home to wait until space became available in the hostel and in the factory.

The day I came home from Allambie Heights, it was Kenny's and my twenty-first birthday. There wasn't a big celebration. We just had a quiet dinner at our place with Wendy, Ken, and their baby, Dwayne. I don't remember where the rest of the family was, although Helene and David drove me home earlier in the day. What I remember most about that night was young Dwayne's finding delight making a noise by banging on the table with a dessert spoon. Dad was still talking about it as he got ready for bed.

In September 1971 Dad and Mum sold the service station business and went on a well-earned trip across the eastern half of Australia. While they were touring, I stayed in a nursing home for three weeks. The best thing that could be said concerning my holiday is that I had a television to myself. Using the knowledge I have now, I can say it wasn't a bad place as nursing homes go.

What disturbed me was that one of the bathrooms was dirty when I first got there, and it was still a disgrace when I left.

When Helene and David asked me back to their place to stay while David worked the night shift, I didn't have to be asked twice. In some ways I felt that I was being left behind when Mum and Dad went away, but I understood that they needed time away from the family. Anyway, that "left behind" feeling wasn't a stranger to me.

In February of the following year, Mum and Dad decided to lease another garage. It was in Fairfield Heights, about thirty-two kilometres from Penrith. This meant moving from Penrith into a flat at Cabramatta. I couldn't quite understand why Mum and Dad were so eager to move out of their new home.

Shifting places didn't worry me too much even though I was confined to the flat and its immediate surrounds most of the time. We were made aware of a sheltered workshop close by, and Dad and I went for an interview with the manager. The attitude again seemed to be, "if you don't have reasonable hand usage, you're not going be much good to us." There was a promise of further contact, but we didn't hear any more from them. Once again I was let down by sheltered employers.

After six or seven months we moved again. This time it was to Fairfield Heights, closer to the business. Soon after we moved, Helene and her two young children came to live with us. She was able to earn an income by working for Dad in the early mornings.

It must have been mid-1973 when Dad was browsing through a newspaper and came across an advertisement for a service station and cafe near Coffs Harbour on the north coast of New South Wales. Mum and Dad always said that, if they ever had the opportunity, they would take the whole family and live by the sea. Dad decided to investigate the possibility further. After notifying the Mobil Company of his interest, he was asked to travel up to have a look at the site. We discovered it was an old place that was being upgraded. The decision was made to lease the business.

The big moving day came. We began the long journey in the late afternoon with all the family's belongings packed into two removalist vans. The trip was done in two stages, and we stayed overnight in a motel at Taree. After beginning the remainder of our trip early the next morning, we reached the small town of Boambee, just south of Coffs Harbour, around midday.

It was fortunate that Mum and Dad had the foresight to rent a flat because, when we arrived, nothing was ready. The cottage, garage, and cafe were half completed. Dad went to work at the unfinished service station almost straight away, but Mum waited until the cafe was ready for business.

Meanwhile, I found it difficult to settle down away from the city. There wasn't much on radio or television, both of which had occupied much of my time back in Sydney.

One Saturday just after the cafe opened, I was left in the flat while Mum and Dad went off to work. It was a gloomy day in more ways than one. Rain fell heavily all day. From about seven o'clock in the morning, I watched the hours slowly tick away while waiting for the test match cricket to start on television. Once the cricket came on, it didn't hold my interest as much as it should have. Two things kept running through my mind. Firstly, I was worried for Mum because I knew that she didn't feel very comfortable about operating a cafe. Second, I was thinking that, if it would only stop raining, I could walk down to visit Kay and her family, who had rented a place in the same street.

After lunch, although I don't remember eating, the situation didn't get any better. I became more restless as the afternoon dragged on and wished the day would end. Early evening came, and I decided to have a shower just to break the boredom. Mum and Dad arrived home to put an end to the worst day that I've ever had. The next day I went to the business with them.

It wasn't long before we could move into the dwelling beside the service station and cafe. This gave the family a whole new lifestyle. It was a twenty-four-hour service station, so Dad, Kenny, and John did a variety of shifts. Mum opened the cafe at five o'clock every morning, and Helene, Kaye, or

Wendy came in to help or to take over from Mum later in the morning. The morning routine for me was to rise out of bed, dress, and wander over to the cafe, where I ate breakfast. I had the pick of the menu.

Shortly after shifting to Coffs Harbour I became homesick for Sydney. This made me write to the Spastic Centre to find out if there was any possibility of moving into their hostel and working at Centre Industries. I can't recall if we received an answer to that particular letter, but farther into my story I did receive a letter.

Not far into 1974 we heard about a sheltered workshop in Coffs Harbour operated by Sheila Russell, who also ran a school. Mum rang Mrs Russell and told her a bit about me. She said to Mum, "Bring him in, and we'll enrol him." I think it was the next day that we went into the workshop. We drove into the driveway that separated the school from the sheltered workplace. We were greeted by Mrs Russell and the supervisor of the workshop.

The main activity was preparing used newspaper and cardboard for recycling. Those people who had reasonable use of their hands would do handcrafts or fold raffle tickets for the local surf-lifesaving clubs. After trying out several jobs, I was given the task of stacking newsprint. This meant piling old newspapers on top of each other until they were about twenty centimetres high. I did this by standing all day, which didn't worry me. However, there was something about the workshop I didn't like. It was basically for people with mental disability—that is, folk with lower than average intelligence or, at worst, mental retardation. In the beginning, I found it a bit strange because the two supervisors in the workshop didn't realise my affliction was only physical. Having a speech problem like mine makes it difficult to convey the level of my intellect. As time went on, they began to see that my mentality was up to par. This was made easier for me when the new supervisor, Mr. Anderson, took charge. He didn't seem to have any preconceived ideas about people with abnormalities, either mental or physical. Despite some childish behaviour that couldn't be helped, everyone was treated like normal adults.

I don't know what things were like before I started, but the workshop gathered momentum as the year went along. Firstly, the building was extended to create more workspace. A press was installed to compact paper and cardboard instead of putting all of the paper in a wool pack held in position by a steel frame and having someone climb up into the wool pack and do something like the stomp dance to make sure it was packed down right.

Then they bought a small truck and employed a driver. He went around to all of the business houses in the district, including our garage, collecting discarded paper and cardboard.

There wasn't always newspaper to stack, so I did other jobs. We had a scrap metal collection going. It involved aluminium drink cans, milk bottle tops, and pie cases. My job was to sort the different thicknesses of the foil.

Christmas 1974 came, and the family looked back on a quite hectic year. At this stage, I think Kenny, Wendy, and the kids had returned to Penrith. Meanwhile, Mum and Dad had to prepare for the busy holiday period ahead. They were told that the tourists would come over the hill on Boxing Day, and that they did.

Poor Mum and Dad were run off their feet for three or four weeks. What made it worst for Mum was that we had visitors staying with us. This meant that, after a very busy day, she had to come home and entertain our guests.

It was a comfortable beginning to the new year. The homesickness finally left me. I had my quadraphonic stereo, and I bought a colour television. Work was quite a pleasant pastime. All things considered, life was running along smoothly. March 5, 1975 came, and it was time to celebrate my twenty-seventh birthday. Among the gifts I received was a letter through the mail from the Spastic Centre asking if I would like to go down for a six-month assessment period at Centre Industries and in the hostel. I was very happy at the prospect of moving back to Sydney. I asked Mum to make the necessary arrangements. This letter should have been the best birthday present I'd ever had, but, unfortunately, things didn't go according to plan.

When all the arrangements were made and it was time to go, something inside my mind said no. I tried to make the move twice, but on each occasion I became nervous and stressed. I wrote to the Spastic Centre again, asking if the offer was still open. They sent a letter back to me suggesting a month's trial. This letter clearly stipulated that, I would have to return home after the trial period. The offer was accepted but not without much distress. Some strange things began running through my mind, such as how I would miss the family, my new television, and my records. Not even the smallest thing escaped my erratic thoughts.

The day prior to going away I was so troubled that I was walking around the house yelling, "I'm not going! I'm not going!" Anyone would have thought it was the end of the world. Mum was sticking to her guns, saying, "You made these arrangements, Max. Now you'll have to go." I became so agitated that I went to a doctor.

That evening Dad, Mum, young Bradley, and I caught the train bound for Sydney. After a good night's rest and breakfast on board, we hired a taxi to go up to Allambie Heights. I can honestly say this was the best month I ever had. There were so many friendly and helpful people around. Everything went so well. I really did have the time of my life. I also enjoyed staying with the people at the hostel, who made me feel very welcome. The assessment period in the factory was much the same as it was in 1969.

At the end of my term, I had to move out of the hostel. Kaye and John picked me up. They were living back in Penrith at the time. The plan was to spend two or three days out there before travelling back to Coffs Harbour. Strangely enough, before leaving home, I had looked forward to those few days with Kaye's family more than the time to be spent at Allambie Heights. As it turned out, the opposite occurred, and that isn't casting any aspersions on the hospitality I received from Kaye and John.

When I unwillingly returned home, it was difficult to settle down. Once again I became restless, but this time the anxiety was because I desperately wanted to get back to the Spastic Centre. However, having spent the month there and knowing what I did, the chances were very slim.

While waiting to return to Sydney, I resumed working at the workshop, much to my dismay.

One Friday afternoon I came home from work feeling so down that I went into my bedroom, lay down on the floor, and began to cry openly. Dad and Mum were in the house at the time. Although they didn't say anything at the time, the next morning it was arranged for me to see the doctor again.

As those weeks passed by, I wrote to the Spastic Centre again, telling them of my despair. They answered by saying it wasn't any longer possible to accommodate me at the hostel. The letter went on to say that, if I wished, a place could be found in a nearby nursing home. Disappointed as I was, I decided to give it a try. I didn't have much choice.

During the first couple weeks in the less-than-favourable living conditions, I slowly grew more agitated at the home and at work. I would be sitting at the workbench, and suddenly all the troubles of the day would spin around in my head, giving me the feeling that I was going mad.

Eventually I went to see the medical staff at Centre Industries. The doctor there monitored my condition, but after a short while he could see that I wasn't improving at all. He then referred me to a specialist, who diagnosed me with depression.

It was New Year's Eve 1975. I had just spent my first Christmas away from home, although Grandma was kind enough to have me at her place for a few days over the festive season. I was sitting in a room in the Plateau View Nursing Home, reflecting on what might have been. Having a dream wrenched from me, I had the feeling that depression would be a part of my life in the future. I felt disappointed in myself because I hadn't grasped a golden opportunity.

As we were getting in the car for the trip back to Collaroy Plateau, Kenny came up to the car door and asked me, "Are you back down at the shelter now, Max?" Of course, there was more to the conversation than that, but I remember those words. The sad part about this was that, in those days, communication between the two of us was practically non-existent. He wouldn't have known what was going on. The next three weeks went smoothly. I was able to strike up a friendship with a young man, Steve, who was in a wheelchair. I also became friendly with his mum and dad.

When I first moved into Plateau View, I was put in a room with an elderly chap. Steve and I put our heads together and decided to ask the matron if we could share the same room, even though we knew that the spare bed in Steve's room belonged to another young man who had gone home for the Christmas break. Steve started the ball rolling by mentioning our plan to a nursing sister. Initially Matron Murphy said to me, "I can't let you have the bed next to Steve because it's Bill's bed," but a couple of days later she changed her mind and said that I could move in with Steve.

Steve's parents were down from Bellingen, which is not far from Coffs Harbour. They were happy to invite me to accompany them on some of their outings. One evening we went to a drive-in theatre, and another day they took me on a trip around Sydney.

Monday came, and it was time to return to work. I had been counting down the days, eager to get on the job. A bus from the Spastic Centre picked up Steve, Bill, and me. At work I was in a section called the Training Unit. This was where people had their assessments done or learned some basic skills before perhaps moving out into the factory.

I was first given the job of countersinking code plates. There were small pieces of metal measuring about three centimetres long, one centimetre wide, and a half centimetre thick. At each end of the plate a hole was punched out, and a hole was drilled in the centre. My job was to remove the burr and leave a small indentation on both sides of the code plates using an air-driven drill fitted to a stand. We had to slide the metal pieces under the drill bit itself and make sure that everything was aligned. A handle was then gently pushed to activate the drill. The machines were set at a particular height so the countersink couldn't be too deep or too shallow. One of the machines had a stop so that, when we slid the code plate beneath the bit, it came to a halt, positioning it correctly for drilling. When the countersunk was finished, a lever would come back up, firing the code plate into a tray. After a couple of months of countersinking, I moved on to tapping the same hole, which involved putting the thread in the centre hole of the code plates using an air-driven machine. It was even more crucial to line up the hole with the tapping bit because, if the bit hit the side of the hole, it would break. There was an added responsibility to keep an eye on the oil flow that cooled the tapping process. After breaking three on the first day, I don't think the supervisor was very pleased with me, but he persevered. I gained confidence and skill as time went by.

One of the great things about working at Centre Industries was that most people had three or four ways of meeting other people. Firstly, there were the folk on board the bus that took us to work. Secondly, there were the people with whom we shared the day at our workplace. Thirdly, we could choose, for the most part, the people we ate with in the canteen. Then there were those people who lived in the two hostels, who were dispersed to every corner of the factory during work time.

My social life really began when I attended the Astra Club, which was held once a month. It was a social club for the workers with cerebral palsy, or "CPs", as we were known in those days. There was a chap, Frank, on our bus who also went along to the Astra Club. The first night I went, Lindsay, the bus driver, who was helping with the club's proceedings, asked Frank and me to the Dee Why RSL for a drink or two. During that year the Astra Club held a couple of cabarets, which were well-attended both by CPs and "Abs" (able-bodied people). Travelling to and from the first one wasn't any trouble for Frank and me. Lindsay kindly volunteered his services, as he lived in the area. This was a very big night, and it was thoroughly enjoyed by all. We danced with everyone to a live band. The second cabaret was just before Christmas, which was also a great occasion. There was a special significance about that night. During the evening Frank asked me to accompany him to Manly League Club to see the Al Martino show. I said I would but expressed concern about my budget. Frank said, "Budgets are meant to be broken."

Frank and I weren't used to going to clubs, so when we arrived dressed in shirtsleeves, we were told that we couldn't attend the show without wearing a coat. When we were seated, an official went away and found two coats for us. We both sat all through the show with these old, battered coats draped around our shoulders. The strange part about that was they relaxed the rules only a couple of weeks later.

This was the night that changed my drinking habits forever—not what I drank, but how I drank. Previously I had drunk with someone holding a cup up to my mouth, or sometimes I would use a cup with two handles. We ordered our Scotch and Cokes. When we got our drinks, they had straws in them. By taking my time sucking on the straw, I found at the end of the night that the glass was empty. I said to Frank, "Who said I couldn't use a straw?" Frank and I enjoyed going to a couple more shows before the year ended. Although I didn't go to many Astra Club gatherings, I look back on it as a vehicle for my social life and the origin of a treasured friendship.

Frank was an intellectual man who had a lively personality. Many people took a liking to him because of his genuine concern for everyone. When I first saw Frank, I thought he was a bit high-class, but as we came to know each other, I found him to be very down-to-earth. The severity level of Frank's cerebral palsy was similar to mine. I think he walked better than I did, but he had limited control over the upper limbs.

1976 was coming to a close, and there were thoughts of going home for the Christmas break. The problem was that the federal government had just brought in a rule that anyone living in a nursing home wasn't allowed any time away. If they did go away, the government subsidy would be stopped. This meant packing up all my belongings and surrendering my bed.

After enjoying the annual leave, I was fortunate to regain a bed at Plateau View. It wasn't far into the New Year when Steve and I were joined by another two young men, Gregory and Rein. Matron Murphy thought it would be a good idea if we were all in one room, as we would be going to work and eating our meals together. This four-bed ward was at the rear of the building, and it was large enough for each of us to carry out our own interests. Someone could be watching television in one corner of the room while another person was listening to the radio in another corner without causing undue disturbance to anyone. We had a large dining table in the centre of the room where we ate our meals. This table was also useful for other activities, such as reading the newspaper.

Living together with the boys was generally enjoyable and harmonious. It sometimes became difficult when one of us—usually me—wanted to go to sleep and when the rest felt like staying awake. I had the only television in the room, and even when there was something that captured the boys' interest on television, I would turn it off, maybe halfway through a show, so I could go to sleep. This didn't give me a great feeling, but what could I do when I needed sleep? The television was left on the nights that I went out.

It was interesting to see how Steve adapted to the new surroundings. While he was in the smaller room, he was often down on the world and difficult to get along with. After the move he was much brighter and joined in with some of our jokes and other pastimes. It wasn't long before Frank and I resumed our night-time jaunts. From the League Club, we decided to broaden our horizons. As the year went on, we patronised Dee Why RSL, the picture theatre at Collaroy, and the Pittwater RSL. The place we visited most frequently was the Pittwater RSL. In addition to the occasional Saturday night, we started to go on a Friday nights. There was a band that played young people's music, which drew a youthful crowd. The club ran a talent quest that proved very popular.

On a Friday the routine was that I would arrive back at the nursing home, have dinner, and prepare for the evening ahead. At about seven o'clock I ordered a taxi to Mona Vale to pick up Frank. Then we would go on to the club. I armed myself with a piece of paper on which there were instructions for the journey. This made it easier for the driver, rather trying to understand what I was saying.

In 1977 Helene married again, and Frank (not be confused with my mate) and she were blessed with Aaron and Michelle.

Sometime during that year I received a promotion at work. This was out into the factory, the machine shop. In this section, the initial forming of the metal components on large lathes and presses was done. The day I was transferred to the machine shop, one of the supervisors from that area came up to the training unit and guided me to my new workplace. Before long I was boring the centre hole in those code plates using a vibrator and an air drill. The vibrator had a round dish mounted above its electric motor. In this dish we loaded forty or fifty code plates, and then the vibration would make them spin around the perimeter. From there they went down a chute and under the drill bit itself. When the code plate was in position, all I had to do was pull down on the handle to drill the hole. After the boring was finished, the code plate was blown out the back of the machine into a steel basket. Then I brought the handle up to its starting point.

It all sounds very easy, but not everything always went according to plan. The machine, which hadn't been used for ages, proved troublesome. The second day on the job I think I broke three drill bits, although this may have been due to my inexperience rather than the machine. The chute that carried the code plates from the vibrator to the drill was made out of thin metal. It was constantly going out of shape and causing the code plates to jam on the way down. The continuous shaking would make the two sections of the machine separate where the chute was attached to the drill. Another problem we learnt to deal with was that, if the code plates hadn't been steam-cleaned, they wouldn't spin around in the vibrator. As time went by we just lived with the trouble this old green machine gave us.

Come pay day, I was pleasantly surprised by how much money I had earned. While working in the training unit, I was earning three or four dollars a week. (I received a pension as well.) My first pay packet after working in the machine shop contained something like sixteen dollars. It increased as the weeks went by, depending how smoothly the machine had run. Back in those days we were paid for what we produced.

The machine shop was, for the most part, a big, corrugated-iron shed. Conditions were very cold in the winter, despite the overhead gas heaters, and it was stifling through the summer months. In fact, there was an in-house rule that stated that, if the temperature went above something like thirty-five degrees, we stopped work. Then we would retreat to the canteen or some other place to quench our thirst. I can remember this happening only once in the four years I worked in this area of the factory. When it rained heavily, water would seep through the roof in a few places.

We heard the news that Matron Murphy was leaving us to have a baby. Quickly the cry went up that "this place won't be the same." Matron Murphy was a thoroughly organised person to whom someone could go with a problem, and she would have it sorted out immediately. She ran the nursing home like it was her own home. If they were short of nurses, she would give a hand, and she took over in the kitchen when the cook or pantry maid didn't come in. She was often seen watering or weeding the garden.

Unfortunately, our worst fears were realised. The place went down after Matron Murphy left. I didn't think that there was anyone reliable enough to give the place a feeling of security.

Early in 1978 I reluctantly returned to Plateau View with the idea firmly in my mind that I would start looking around for another nursing home. Meanwhile, things went from bad to worse. Upon my return I found Gregory had left, and the bed had been taken by an elderly man. The new matron had the idea that she would move the four of us to the front of the building near the main entrance. (Strange how history repeats itself.)

The reason given for the relocation was that "it looks better than old people sitting around all day." There were a couple of problems. The first one was this elderly chap. He had a chest complaint and said he needed all the fresh air possible. This meant we had to keep all the windows and blinds and the door wide open. We were denied privacy when changing.

The other problem we had was that the new ward was near a room that had a television in it. The sisters' station was close by, so there wasn't much quiet when we were trying to sleep.

One night I came home after celebrating becoming a member of the Dee Why RSL. Frank, two of our bus drivers, and I all went on this evening out, so we made a bit of noise when we arrived back at the nursing home. A few days later I was explaining my unhappiness in my current surroundings to the new matron, as I had done before. She brought up the fact that we were noisy that night. I thought to myself, "There goes my argument." The staff knew I didn't like being in that room, and most of them changed their attitude towards me; where once they were friendly and showed interest in what I did, suddenly I was out of favour. This gave me a feeling of rejection— something I wasn't used to—and it felt awful.

Eventually I was switched back into a two-bed room with an elderly man. I think this decision was made with the influence of a nursing sister to whom I had spoken. She was among the few people who were on my side. This support was discovered when I asked to use the phone to ring Mum and Dad and tell them that I wanted to come home.

In September of that year, Mum and Dad sold their business and bought a small property in Bonville, which is about ten kilometres south of Coffs Harbour. It was an older-style two-bedroom house with a full-length patio at the front and a closed-in veranda at the back. The outside of the house was imitation red brick with a green corrugated roof. The homestead was in a rural setting on the summit of a hill. We had a view down over fields where cattle and horses grazed or people had sown various crops. Beyond the farmlands were hills covered with banana plantations.

At times the countryside looked beautiful, particularly when it had been raining and the mist hung above the landscape. At sunset after a fine day, the clouds became colourful as that ball of fire sneaked behind the hills.

Mum and Dad leased the Seabreeze Milk Bar early in 1979. It was at Sawtell, which is between Coffs Harbour and Bonville. This created a new interest for me, as I would go to the shop and watch the passing parade. On a few occasions I ventured a short stroll to the beach with Mum and Dad's approval.

In February I got a bed at Ocean View Nursing Home, where Frank lived. I caught the overnight coach to Sydney, although I can't remember in which part of the city I disembarked. Then I hired a taxi and travelled out to

Mona Vale. When I arrived at the nursing home at about seven o'clock that morning, Frank was waiting at the door for me. After a friendly greeting we went inside, and I was shown my bed. While Frank went off to work, I settled into my new abode.

This was a well-run nursing home because the management had been there for a long while. It was a strange administration as nursing homes go. There was a matron who was in charge and looked after the day-to-day proceedings, at least while I was there. At the same time a husband-and-wife owner team kept a close eye on whatever happened in the place.

Frank and I were able to make the most of going out. Ocean View is on Pittwater Road, one of the main arteries of Sydney. We could walk down to the bus stop and go to our League or RSL Clubs without having the expense of taxis. Sometimes we would compromise, going part of the way by cab and the rest by bus. Occasionally we ventured on a Saturday night into Sydney, getting off the bus at Wynyard Railway Station and strolling towards George Street. In those days it had a very adult theme. Various small theatres exhibited X-rated pictures, and in between they ran live shows. I don't think it would be giving away any secrets if I said Frank and I attended just a couple of those shows! There were nights when we caught a bus to Kings Cross, where we walked up and down the footpath, taking in the sights. Again it would be wrong to say we didn't see the odd strip show. One thing that always amazed me about "The Cross" is how many people it drew.

The Saturday before Easter we went to The Royal Easter Show. It was the first time that I'd been. Frank said that, when his mother was alive, they would go a couple of times whenever the show was on. We asked a friend, Ian, to come along and assist us through the day.

We all caught a bus into Wynyard and then a cab out to the showground. After spending some time wandering around looking at the various displays (although I can't recall just what we saw), we decided to have lunch. After we had eaten, Ian told us he had to meet someone at the entrance of the grounds. He went away and then returned without his friend. This happened three or four times.

By the time Ian found his mate, Frank and I had been in the same place for four hours, and we weren't very pleased. After we finally regrouped, we had just enough time to have more to eat and then begin thinking about making our way back home. I must say it was a very disappointing day all around.

Ian had a mild case of cerebral palsy, so he could drive a car. Towards the end of 1979, Frank and Ian began renting cars for a day or for the weekend. I think my first trip with them was into Sydney. Ian drove while Frank gave directions. At times it was a bit frightening sitting in the back seat.

The year was quickly coming to a close. Once again I had to put all my belongings together and move out of the nursing home.

The plan was to have three or four weeks at home and then return to Ocean View. It didn't turn out that way. When it came time to reapply for a bed, they kept saying there wasn't one available. It became obvious after a number of telephone calls to the nursing home that they wouldn't have me back. Why weren't they honest enough to tell us I didn't have a chance of regaining my bed? Meanwhile, Frank and Ian flew up to the Gold Coast for a while during the Christmas break. They decided to rent a car for the homeward journey. On the way back they called in to see me, and I introduced them to Dad. Some of my nephews and nieces were around too. Unfortunately, Mum was at work. We had a leisurely chat over a beer or two. All too soon it was time for them to make tracks again.

It was heading towards March when we asked the Spastic Centre to become involved with my accommodation situation. They recommended a place in Strathfield, the Helenville Nursing Home. I knew that six or eight people from Centre Industries had just moved into the home. It seemed to me that the Centre, along with the owners, had the idea of converting the place into a young people's hostel. While it wasn't really the area I wanted to live in, I decided to try it.

Dad, Mum, and I drove down from Coffs Harbour, arriving at my new home in the midafternoon. We found an old house that had been converted into a nursing home. The large rooms were used as wards, with elderly folk and young people in together. I was put into a six-bed ward with three other young men. Two of them had shared the ward at Plateau View. Again I found my mates good to be with, as were the other young people in the place.

However, there were some things about Helenville that I found unacceptable and alarming. It was very disturbing to find how little trained staff were at Helenville. We would have one nurse's aide on afternoon shift for nineteen patients, followed by another nurse's aide on night duty. True enough: the matron lived on the premises when I first moved in, but soon after she went into a private dwelling.

The building itself was badly designed for a nursing home, in my opinion. There were steps at the front and rear entrance. I can't remember just where the wheelchair access was. An interior step divided the two wards from the rest of the home, so anyone in a self-propelled wheelchair was limited in their movements without assistance.

We had great concern about the food supply at Helenville. Clearly, there wasn't enough food to either satisfy the needs of young people or suit the fees we were paying. These fees were comparable to any other nursing home around Sydney at the time. To give an idea of what I mean, I will compare breakfast at Ocean view to breakfast at Helenville.

Breakfast at Ocean view was a bowl of cereal, a plate full with bacon, sausages, and eggs or the like, along with two slices of toast with jam or marmalade, and a pot of tea or coffee.

Breakfast at Helenville was a bowl of cereal, one slice of bread and butter, and a cup of tea. Occasionally we had a boiled egg or a poached egg on toast.

During the stay in Strathfield, my social life didn't suffer much. For the first time in my life, I was catching trains. Frank would ring and ask me if I wanted to see a movie or do something else in Sydney. It took ten or fifteen minutes for me to stroll up to Strathfield railway station. From there I would catch a train to Wynyard station and meet Frank. I ventured up to the northern beaches to Mona Vale a few times. One Sunday I decided to visit

Frank. I wandered up to Strathfield station, caught the train to Wynyard, and boarded a bus to Mona Vale. After a pleasant journey, I arrived at Ocean View only to find that Frank had gone out five minutes before. I had to make my way back home. The round trip took over three hours.

Another day I was going somewhere and had to catch a train to Wynyard. Somehow I hopped aboard the wrong train. The next thing I knew, the train was heading towards Hornsby, which is northwest of Sydney. Fortunately, I was able to explain my predicament to a guard, who organised the train to stop at a particular station, or it may have been a scheduled set down.

After four months at Helenville, I went home feeling disappointed with those who ran the place and the people who had recommended it to me. I also felt for those young folk who remained in the nursing home. During the period at Helenville, I spent a lot of time trying to find more desirable accommodation for myself.

Upon returning home, I wrote a letter to the board of directors at the Spastic Centre, explaining my concerns about Helenville. This letter was complete with typing errors and spelling mistakes, but we received a reply stating that the board had carefully noted down everything that I had to say. I don't know whether this changed much at Helenville, but it made me feel better to have written to give my point of view—and I felt even better when there was an answer.

While I was at Helenville, I wrote to Peninsular Gardens Nursing Home at Mona Vale. It was a place I had known about for a few years. A couple of weeks before Christmas, Mum had a phone call from this particular nursing home saying that there was a bed available. Since it was Christmas, we tried to stave off my departure from home, but they wanted the bed filled, no doubt for financial reasons. I flew back down to Sydney with "I'll try it again" running through my mind. I was hoping for a long-term arrangement with a nursing home. Grandma, Auntie Mary, and Uncle Colin picked me up from the airport. Colin had some time on his hands, as he was between barber-shop ownerships. It was great to see them. Grandma was concerned about the lack of space to store my belongings, but as I said in a thank you note to them, everything fit with room to spare.

Peninsular Gardens provided me with very comfortable living accommodations. The staff made me feel much at home by taking a great interest in my life.

A couple of days after settling in, not wishing to resume work until the new year, I asked Sister Griffith if it was all right to go across to the beach. It was only about a hundred metres to walk, and the jaunt quickly became a favourite pastime. I would stroll over with my beach towel, sit on the sand, and watch everything that went on. I'd never seen so many undressed female bodies in my life! I was really in my element! Occasionally I ventured into the surf. Getting down on my hands and knees to crawl to the water, I would wait until the waves brought the water up to me, rather than going out too far. Thinking back, this may have been foolhardy because I never surfed between the flags. There were too many people, and I was frightened of being knocked over.

A couple of weeks after Christmas, I returned to work and continued my duties in the machine shop. The friends I'd made over the years gave me a big welcome back.

The declaration of 1981 as the International Year of Disabled Persons was an important catalyst in the process of increasing the community's awareness of the situation of handicapped people in Australia. A generic consequence was that the term "people with disabilities" became more widely used instead of the individual name of an affliction. In addition, during 1981 the Anti-Discrimination Act was amended to make it unlawful to discriminate on grounds of physical impairment.

In New South Wales at least, there were special toilet facilities in public areas provided for people with disabilities. The Taxi Transport Subsidy Scheme used specially modified taxis for people with disabilities so they could remain in their wheelchairs, rather than transferring to the seat of the cab. This scheme works with a docket system: when we reach the end of a journey, we give the taxi driver half of the fare in cash, and the other half is documented and sent to the state government. People with less severe disabilities are able to take full advantage of this system by catching a normal cab.

Another result of the Year of Disabled People was the provision for disabled car spaces in the community. These areas are set aside for drivers with a disability or for passages in the car with a disability. The vehicle must display a special sticker.

The Department of Housing in New South Wales began modifying dwellings as necessary for disabled tenants. These houses have greatly decreased the number of young people with disabilities who must live in nursing homes and hostels.

Although not involving myself much in the celebrations or politics of the Year of Disabled People, I played one small part at Centre Industries. It was decided to set up some committees to represent various sections of the Spastic Centre. Hoping to win a place on the central committee and after being nominated, I mounted a campaign based on my past experiences with nursing homes. This may have been foolish of me, considering that I was still living in a nursing home, as good as it was. I wrote down all the misgivings I thought young people who were staying in those places had and made it my platform for election. Complete with typing errors and spelling mistakes, this document was pinned up on the notice boards throughout Centre Industries. A few days before voting day, I circulated a reminder with my name, something about nursing homes, and my slogan, "Vote Stone for a rock solid representation." When the big day came, every CP had an opportunity to elect his or her committee member for a twelve-month period.

In the committee room I stayed on the fringe of any deep discussion or decision-making, not because I didn't have an interest in what was being said but because I've always found it difficult to take in a conversion with a large group of people. Most of the time I was there just making up the quorum.

Otherwise, the year went along very well. The staff at Peninsular Gardens showed their continued support for me. Frank and I celebrated my thirty-third birthday at the Pittwater RSL Club with five or six staff members from the home.

Christmas came creeping up once again. Joan, one of the night nurses asked me what I would be doing during the holiday break. I explained to her the situation concerning the extra money that I would have to pay if I left the nursing home for a few days.

Just before Christmas I received a gift from seven staff members. It was a return air ticket to Coffs Harbour. I was overjoyed by such generosity.

After an enjoyable week at home, I returned to Peninsular Gardens on New Year's Day. The next three weeks were filled with trips to the beach and relaxing. One particular day stands out in my mind. Debbie, a young nursing sister who came to work at Peninsular Gardens and whom I had come to know when she worked at Ocean View, also frequently visited Mona Vale Beach. It was a Monday morning at about ten o'clock when I decided to go across to the beach and sunbathe. As I walked onto the beach, I noticed Debbie lying on her stomach with her head turned towards the path that led onto the sand. She saw me and invited me over. I spread my towel out, and Debbie helped with one corner. I lay beside her on my back. We chattered away for a while. Something caught my attention on the beach, which made me look elsewhere for a while. Then my eyes wandered back to where Debbie was lying. She had silently rolled over onto her back. This made me feel like a king because Debbie always sunbathed without a bikini top, and she was "well stacked." It gave me an enormous sense of pride to think she trusted my seeing usually a private part of her body and making it such an intimate situation. All too soon my morning came to an end when Debbie reminded me it was nearly lunchtime back at the nursing home. I left the beach that day, thrilled at having been a part of Debbie's morning.

It was time to return to work after having the best summer of my life. I remember telling someone, "Life is going so well for me and looks like staying that way." So it did for the first three months of the year. Then out of the blue came the news that the fees at Peninsular Gardens were going up by twenty dollars a week. That was twenty dollars above my pension, and I couldn't afford it since I was earning only eight or ten dollars a week. This happened right at Easter. It somewhat spoiled what otherwise may have been a great long weekend. After a lot of umming, arghing, and totalling the bank balance, I found no alternative other than to go home. It was very upsetting that my life had to be put on hold just because the government would allow a nursing home to change their fees so much. It didn't affect only me; there were some elderly folk, too, who had to find other accommodations.

On the Tuesday after Easter, there was a farewell party held for me at the Mona Vale hotel. Ten or twelve people from the nursing home attended the gathering. I was presented with a silver bracelet.

The following Sunday Kenny and Uncle Ross drove me to the airport for the flight home. I was amazed at how quickly I was able to settle down. After a few weeks I was feeling right at home, resigned to the fact that I would be at home for quite a while.

The spring before, Dad had planted a hundred or so fruit trees. There were about sixty nectarine trees, and the remainder were various varieties of peach trees. This became a great interest for Dad and me. We spent hours walking through the small orchard, just watching them grow. Sometimes, when Dad was at work, I spent hours dragging a hose around from tree to tree, hoping to give them enough water to bear quality fruit.

When it came picking time the first year, we discovered a few problems. One disappointment was the birds that came and pecked at the peaches. They didn't attack the nectarines so much. One afternoon Dad came home to find a tree stripped of its fruit and leaves. Another menace was flying foxes, otherwise known as fruit bats. They came down at night, and once again the peaches were the prime target. As some of the trees reached maturity, they developed a disease called canker, which causes an open wound in the stem of a tree.

Our first big harvest was in the spring of 1983. We were surprised at how much fruit came from what were not much more then seedlings. The second year Dad bought a motorised spraying machine, rather than using a small snap sack. This saw me standing beside a two-hundred-litre drum with a stick, stirring the bluestone and lime so it wouldn't settle at the bottom. While I was doing that, Dad went around to each tree, giving it a spray.

Mum had a weekend job working in a kitchen of a nursing home, so she left home at five thirty in the morning. Dad would drive her into Coffs Harbour and then return home to prepare breakfast for the two of us. He also assisted me with morning tea and lunch.

During the first year I was at home, I wrote a paper on the experiences I'd had in nursing homes. It turned out to be a five-page document.

The introduction read:

> A shortage of proper hostel accommodation around Sydney makes it necessary for some of us to live in nursing homes.
>
> Sometimes these places are found by a sheltered employer or rehabilitation groups, and sometimes they're sought by our own means. Either way, the fact is that some of these places are much better run and far more suitable for young handicapped adults than others.
>
> I share some of my experiences of living in four nursing homes over the last six years. This is done in a truthful and, I hope, a constructive way to show what may happen when a handicapped person chooses a nursing home or, importantly, has no alternatives.

Then I went through the various experiences, similar to what has been done earlier in my story.

The conclusion read:

> To close this paper, I would like to say something generally about nursing homes, the people who run them, and those who recommend them.

When people seek admission or re-admission to a nursing home, it is sometimes the practice for the nursing home to say, "Yes, we will put your name on our waiting list." Six or twelve months later, they are still waiting and often in vain. I consider this practice to be without good reason. It also can be a hindrance for making other plans. This has happened to me more than once.

I find it difficult to accept that young, handicapped people should be placed into substandard living when often the fees are comparable to those charged by far better accommodations.

If sheltered employers or rehabilitation groups are going to be in the business of recommending nursing homes, they should make sure that these places are of a very high standard. We want the best for our money at all times. I think it is a very sad reflection on those who recommend nursing homes and their resources when I can find better accommodation than they can.

I consider it wrong when nursing homes are permitted to raise their fees so much above the basic pension rate that some people can't afford to remain in them.

It seems to me that, if enough proper hostels can't be provided for young handicapped people, it is time for governments, nursing home authorities, and handicapped welfare groups to all come together. Then maybe a policy could be formulated whereby a person could live in a nursing home of his or her choice without having to fear low living standards or suddenly having to pay charges that can't be met.

For all the effort I put into writing this paper, it didn't see the light of day.

As in days gone by, I was kept occupied by watching television. I became a big fan of *The Mike Walsh Show*. For a short time, dare I say, some of the soapies grabbed my interest.

Then there were my records, and by that time I had a collection of cassettes that I started with the move back to Sydney. It proved to be easy to carry a small cassette player. Moving into the video age created another interest for me. Being an early-to-bed person, I would record the late night shows and watch them the next day, and, of course, I could hire the latest movies.

Frank and Ian drove up to see us on the Anzac weekend of 1983, arriving late Friday afternoon. After we all caught up over dinner with what everyone had been doing, we spent the evening watching the Logie Awards. It was a good thing that Mum didn't have to work the next morning because Ian persuaded us to stay up until the alternate accolade was announced.

The boys and I went into Coffs Harbour on Saturday morning to buy a connection lead for my stereo. We thought they might have it at Tandy. Frank heard on the radio that the Beatnix (Beatles impersonators) were going be performing at the Sawtell RSL Club. When he mentioned it to us, Dad, a member of the club, was able to arrange tickets for the show.

What a band! Anyone who is familiar with the sound of the Beatles really couldn't fault the performance of these four men. I've seen them more recently, and they haven't lost any authenticity. We had Beatles music ringing in our ears that weekend because Frank brought some tapes up for me to record.

One family that Frank and Ian hadn't met was Kaye and John and their two children, so on Sunday we went into Coffs Harbour to visit them. John rolled the welcome mat out by offering us a beer. The only blemish on the day was that we were late back for lunch, and Mum had prepared a hot meal. She wasn't pleased about having to keep the food warm.

Frank thought he had a distant relative living nearby, so on Monday morning Ian had a look in the local telephone book and found that they lived in Sawtell. After making a phone call to confirm they were the right people and were happy to have visitors, we were on our way. We were invited to stay for lunch and try the new microwave. Monday afternoon came, and all too soon it was time for Frank and Ian to return home.

The following Easter I was able to fly down to Sydney to spend a week or so with them. This was possible because, during that past year, Frank had been discharged from Ocean View and admitted to hospital to have a spinal operation. Rather than moving back into a nursing home, Frank and Ian decided to rent a flat together, using the Homecare service. Someone would come in morning and night to prepare the meals and give personal care to Frank. By this time, they had also bought a car, which made it easier to go places. They picked me up from the airport for the trip back to their place on Thursday evening.

After a restful night and a late sleep-in, Good Friday began in an eventful way. We were sitting around the breakfast table enjoying hot-cross buns when suddenly Frank started coughing with a piece of bun caught in his throat. Ian jumped up from the chair and tried to apply the Heimlich manoeuvre, but with no result. Then he quickly rang the ambulance. It wasn't long coming, although by that time Frank had recovered. The ambulance officers asked him if he was all right or if he wanted to be taken to hospital for further observation. Frank chose the latter. I remained at the flat while Ian drove the car behind the ambulance. Shortly after they arrived at the hospital, Ian rang me to say everything was fine. Frank just had to stay for a few hours for observation. Ian later explained to us that he saw the Heimlich manoeuvre done in a movie. I thought it was quick thinking on his part, regardless of the result.

We covered a lot of ground in the ten days I was there. Apart from going into Sydney a couple of times, we went down to Wollongong and visited Frank's relatives. We went out to Penrith and saw Grandma. I hadn't seen her since she had moved into a new home. We were all surprised how large the house was. The boys said it would make a wonderful house for people with disabilities, if only it were closer to work. We enjoyed afternoon tea with Grandma's famous scones. Well, they're famous to the family, anyway.

Frank and Ian went to work a few days while I was there, so it gave me a chance to venture out on my own. The flat was in a central part of Dee Why, which made it easy to catch a bus. One of the trips took me back to Peninsular Gardens, where I saw some old friends. I even went on a nostalgic stroll across to the beach. Another day I went up to Centre Industries to see my mates.

Towards the end of 1984 I heard from Frank that there was a new matron at Ocean View. I wrote to her to see what response I would get, if any. To my surprise we received a phone call in January from the manager, who said that they had a bed for me.

On the following Sunday we rang Frank and Ian to tell them the good news. Mum asked if they would mind picking me up from the airport, and they obliged willingly. I arrived in Sydney in the late afternoon. After sharing a meal with the boys, we got to the nursing home around eight o'clock. We were greeted by Sister Martin, whom we all knew. She was there for most of Frank's stay, and I met her in 1979. It seemed Betty had plenty of time for Frank and me. We thought the world of her. I was put into a two-bed room at first, but that didn't last long. Within two or three weeks they gave me a single room with an en suite. My first reaction was to ask, "How can I afford this?" In days gone by, if anyone went into a single or a private room of a nursing home, he or she would have to pay much more than the basic rate, so when the matron explained that all the rooms had the same low fee, I was pleasantly surprised.

My aim, of course, was to return to Centre Industries, but I found out that they wanted to do a new assessment. I suppose there was a need to update the records because of the long break. The morning I went back came as a huge shock to me. After reporting to the assessment officer, who wrote down some particulars, we started to walk out of the rehabilitation area and down through the old machine shop. We entered a large room that had once been off limits for people without authority. In this area people were packing items into boxes, putting leaflets in envelopes, assembling desk lamps, sticking on foam rubber ear guards, and doing various other jobs that had been brought in from outside companies.

Within a couple of days I sadly realised that it wasn't the same old Centre Industries I had come to know. The factory was still operating, but it was slowly winding down.

At the end of my nine-day period, I stayed back at the nursing home, waiting for the word to return to work. During that two or three weeks, something happened to me of which I couldn't make any sense. Depression set in, and I really didn't know why, considering things were going my way. Over a few days I felt myself slowly slipping down.

A sure sign for me when depression is approaching is when I get a tight feeling in my chest or when my eyes feel like I've been crying. In fact, an end result of my depressed periods has been bursting into tears. Other than the embarrassment, this crying often comes as a great release. This meant going back to the specialist. I have often asked myself, "Why me? Why do I have to put up with the anxiety? Haven't I got enough to contend with in life?" The only explanation I've heard is that it has to do with chemicals in the body.

I often went to Dee Why to visit Frank and Ian. One of the first places we went that year was into Sydney to watch the Gay and Lesbian Mardi Gras. We couldn't see much of the march because of the large crowd. To make an uneventful night worse, I had a fall and landed on some gravel, scratching my face. The next day saw me feeling very sore and sorry for myself. This was the first of two tumbles early that year.

The second fall was when I went down to Dee Why RSL Club one Saturday night. As I stepped off the bus, I fell onto a steel manhole cover, and that meant more skin off my face. I hurried into the club's men's room to inspect the damage. A peep in the mirror told me it wasn't a good look. I wet a handkerchief to wipe some of the blood off. The thought ran through my mind that perhaps I should go home straight away.

Deciding to stay, I made my way to the auditorium to watch the floor show and met a bloke I worked with. Winton didn't notice—or at least he didn't mention—the state of my face. After seeing quite a good show and enjoying a couple of beers, I thought it would be wise to order a cab rather than catching the bus. This didn't provide me with much protection. I returned to Ocean View only to have another fall. This time, I got out of the taxi, walked towards the front door, and went straight into the flower garden. It wasn't clear how much more damage was done to my face, but I decided to blame it on the last tumble.

In July the nursing home changed matrons. One of the first things the new Director of Nursing (DON), as she liked to be called, tried was to stop me from using public transport. Well-meaning, as I'm sure she was, she was trying to look out for my safety, but the truth was that I couldn't afford to catch taxis everywhere.

At the time, Centre Industries had a department known as Support Services. Among the staff in this office were several social workers. I explained the situation to one of them, and she rang the DON back at Ocean View, who stood firm on her decision.

Meanwhile, I thought of the idea of asking Mum and Dad to write a letter to the nursing home, stating that they gave their permission for me to catch a bus. I don't know whether the letter changed the DON's mind or it was the pressure put on her by the social worker, or maybe it was the combination of both, but she took me aside one morning before I went to work and said, "Sorry if I caused you any distress. You can go on the buses again."

When I told the social worker of the good news, she was happy for me. "Now I won't have to send the letter I've written to the Anti-discrimination Board. It was such a good letter, too," she said.

There was another issue shortly after that episode. Frank, Ian, and I were going to Sydney's Entertainment Centre to see the Everly Brothers. The show was on midweek. Rather than rushing home from work, I had the day off to prepare for the big night ahead.

When the deputy matron, who hadn't been at Ocean View long, came on duty and heard that I was having a "sicky", she sent a nursing sister around to my room to find out what was happening. I explained the situation. The next thing I knew, they had rung work to find out if it was all right for me to have a day off.

Christmas came around once again, but this time I didn't have to go through the task of packing up. The government had brought in a new rule saying that anyone who was staying in a nursing home could spend twenty-eight days away from the place and not lose their subsidy. This suited me well.

One of the highlights of 1986 was meeting Sharon and Julia. Both were nurses. Sharon came to work at Ocean View, and Julia worked in another nursing home nearby. An instant rapport was established among the three of us. This was made easier for the girls because, when they lived in Queensland, they had a friend who had cerebral palsy. I went out with them a few times. One Sunday we decided to go to Sydney's Luna Park. I don't remember exactly what we did. I know we rode on a ghost train, and Sharon had a ride on a pirate ship. We had chicken for lunch, and on the way home we stopped for a pizza.

Sharon walked around the ground all day with bare feet. She was a tough girl and swore like a trooper, but I didn't mind seeing that side of her. She hated my calling her butch. The main thing for me was that Sharon had a heart of gold.

It may be wrong of me to compare the two girls, but I found Julia was very much a lady. She had style and class and also immense generosity. Both girls at that stage insisted they were meant for each other, which in some ways made me left out in the cold.

They invited me to stay at their flat for a weekend, and I really enjoyed myself. We began with an evening at the Pittwater RSL Club. On Saturday we went up to the Central Coast to visit Julia's relatives. While there, we stopped at the Reptile Park. The girls' interest was captured by the young joeys in the kangaroos' pouches. They spent a long time trying to find them. Sharon and Julia weren't around long before they decided to enrol in a nursing course at a college near Hornsby. This meant moving from the Mona Vale area and into student accommodations, but that didn't mean the end of our friendship. The girls called in every so often. After their yearlong course, they invited me to the graduation. Unfortunately, I lost contact with Sharon about three years later, when she went back to New Zealand. Julia returned to Queensland but, when travelling down this way, she always drops in to see me, even after nearly a decade.

There was another lady of whom I became rather fond, but this time the admiration was all one way. Wendy was a night nurse. She assisted me in dressing for work some mornings. Wendy was a fairly short person with a lovely figure, or at least I thought so. I really found her attractive. She said a couple of things to me that made me feel on top of the world.

I have come to realise that, when someone has a disability like mine, he or she can't be very attractive to the average able-bodied person, even when he or she presents a positive image. While understanding this to a tee, it doesn't at all quell the desire to take part in the natural pleasure of making love. I have spent many nights lying awake, just wondering what it would feel like to give love and receive love both emotionally and physically. There are times when this desire becomes a real need.

The Royal Far West Children's Health Scheme and Services for the Aged bought and took over the running of Ocean View Nursing Home as part of their investment strategy. This meant a gradual upgrade of the place over the next few years.

Halfway through the year I became involved with a hydrotherapy programme at Centre Industries. There was an indoor heated swimming pool at the rear of the factory that I hadn't seen before. Once a fortnight or so, a group of six people with disabilities, along with ladies from the physiotherapy department, would go down to have a splash.

We couldn't jump in the pool and do what we liked. It was an organised exercise session. Each lady took one disabled person, and after one or two warm-up laps, we played pass-the-parcel, dived for rings that were thrown into the bottom of the pool for us to retrieve, and do various other activities. The off-the-chill water was invigorating, although I swallowed litres of it.

After I spent almost seven weeks off work and enjoyed most of that period at home with Mum and Dad, it was time to settle into 1987. Early in the year the DON asked me if I would like to move into a private room with a door that opened onto a balcony. The move was welcome. It gave me more of chance to enjoy the outdoors. I often took a transistor radio out and sat in the sun for hours.

Nearly all through the year, there wasn't much work for me to do. It became so quiet that I took my electric typewriter to work and began taking a short story course. This continued until quite late into the year, when our workgroup was broken up. A couple of us were placed on a bench where door and window locks were packed. There were about twelve people working on the line. At one end of the table were laid six plastic blisters side by side in a shallow box. The box was slid to each person to drop in a particular component, such as keys, screws, and the lock itself. After the box had gone around to everyone, it finished up where it had started. Then the loaded blisters were lifted out onto a heat-sealing machine, which would mould on the cardboard backs.

Frank had another operation on his spine. Ian and I often visited him at Royal North Shore hospital, and later Frank was moved out to Lady Davison Repatriation Hospital at Turramurra. Ian and I always found it amazing how Frank stayed in such high spirits. If we went to visit him with a group of people, he made a special point of speaking to everyone individually.

The greatest surprise of 1987 was receiving a telephone call from Kenny one Saturday night, saying he would come down to see me the next day. When he arrived, we decided to go out and headed off in the car. Then Kenny asked me if I would like to go to the rugby league semi-final at the Sydney Cricket Ground. We thought catching a bus would be the best way to go. We had great pleasure seeing our team, Penrith, winning their under-21s match.

Along with the visit came an invitation to spend the next weekend with Kenny, but I declined the offer after Kenny made big plans. We spoke about celebrating our fortieth birthdays together the following March.

I can look back on the holiday period of 1987–1988 as being nearly perfect— at least until the very last day. There was a robbery at Ocean View, and I was one of the victims. One Sunday I was sitting out in the sun. Lunchtime came around, and I was asked if I would like to eat outside, rather than returning to my room. One of the agency nurses they sometimes bring in when someone calls in sick was assisting me with my meal. These are often people we've never seen before. When I'd finished the meal, I needed a straw to have a drink. The nurse went to my room, which was quite a distance from where I was sitting. She seemed to take longer than she should have, but she came back and I didn't think any more of it. Later that afternoon I went to my wallet and found fifty dollars had been taken. I reported it to a nursing sister. Then I was told that several other people had been robbed. One dear old lady had eighty dollars' worth of two-dollar coins wrapped up, and they were stolen.

There have been a number of robberies at Ocean View over the years since I've lived in the place. Three times I've been a victim. This led me to obtain a key card so I would have to keep only small amounts of money at hand. After the last theft and maybe a long time after I should have, I had a lock fitted to my chest of drawers.

When we have to rely on other people for personal assistance, we are open to all kinds of treatment. Living in a nursing home for as long as I have is testimony to that. Over the years I've seen it all, from the very good to the very bad and everything in between. Some people take real pride in their work and make you feel like a real person. Other people have an "anything will do" attitude. Some people choose to do the bare minimum and haven't any compassion at all. There have been occasions when someone has walked into my room to help me and asked me to change the channel on my television or the music I'm playing. This irritates me greatly. I think it's like my walking into someone's lounge room and asking them to change what they were watching or listening to. As in the wider community, different people react differently to a person with a disability. Some people can't differentiate a physical from a mental disability. They seem to think that the two go hand in hand. Other people are willing to give the benefit of the doubt.

As I said earlier, it's not easy to make intelligent conversation with someone who has speech impairment. Some people have very little difficulty understanding what I'm saying. Other people have problems understanding what I'm saying, try as they may. I don't mind their persevering with me. I would much rather people do that than pretend to understand me. I can always tell when I'm not being understood, and there are people who haven't the time or patience to listen.

March came around, and I went to Gosford to spend the weekend with Kenny and Wendy. Kenny picked me up on Friday evening. On Saturday morning Kenny and I went on a boat cruise at the Brisbane Waters. In the afternoon we went to the new Erina Fair shopping Centre, where we saw some magnificent skateboarding.

Party time came, and there were relatives from Wendy's side of the family. Kenny and I were the only members from our clan, which was disappointing. I would have liked at least to have seen Mum and Dad there. The highlight of the evening was Wendy's brother Warren and his quick wit. He made us all laugh constantly.

On Sunday morning we went to buy plants for some hanging pots that Mum had given me. I had also received a planter pole the previous Christmas from a friend and hadn't yet assembled it.

In the afternoon Kenny asked me if I wanted to go to church with him. I was surprised at how much he had become involved in his religion. Whether it influenced him to come see me I don't know, but ever since the initial visit, not many weeks have gone by without Kenny coming down or giving me a phone call. Now I have a brother who can't do enough for me and a real mate.

In June I was elected to C I Council, which was similar to the old committee of 1981. I don't know how my election came about because I didn't remember anyone's asking if he or she could nominate me, and I definitely didn't run any campaign.

Once again it was difficult to take part. However, a couple of months into it, I became involved with the recreation sub-committee that was part of a new department the Spastic Centre had set up to look after the recreational needs of people with disabilities. The purpose of the sub-committee was to direct the activities of the recreation programme. Volunteering for the secretary's position was a whole new experience. I sat through meetings, and then one or two days later I typed up the minutes using the agenda and my memory to guide me. I chaired several meetings while our liaison officer was away.

The disappointing part about having these meetings was that the recreation officer would not work with us. In the end we were just going through the motions of having a meeting, as what we said or did had no effect on the recreation programme at all.

In the latter half of that year my niece Jodie gained a position at Commonwealth Bank at Manly. It felt good to have a member of the family living so close, although visits were rare.

Frank moved into government housing after living in one of the Spastic Centre hostels as he recovered from an operation. The house was at Naraweena, just west of Dee Why. Shortly after he settled in, I went to see him one Saturday afternoon. The house was impressive. Frank was sharing the house with another man, Albert, but shortly after they moved in, Albert went home for a weekend, never to be seen again.

Frank asked me to consider moving in with him. It didn't take long to decide to stay where I was because I really cherished our friendship and didn't want to jeopardise it.

Going up to Frank's place became a regular Saturday afternoon outing for me. We always had a good talk about several things. Frank always insisted that I have dinner with him and was always disappointed when it was time for me to leave.

Another nurse who came to work at Ocean View, Debbie, took a liking to me, and we really enjoyed each other's company. She asked me to her home to have a meal with her, her husband, and her young son.

One of the best nights we had was when we went with another couple to the Sydney Entertainment Centre to see John Farnham. Among the other places Debbie and I went was Darling Harbour in Sydney about Australian history. This outing came about because I had gone to an exhibition with a social club the weekend before and didn't see much at all. I told Debbie how much I missed out on. She agreed with me that I should have seen more, so she offered to spend a whole day at the show.

Another day, we went out for lunch. I was telling Debbie how, one night at the nursing home, they had left me waiting for some length of time before answering my buzzer. At the end of my story, Debbie had a tear in her eye. Debbie and I had many good times together.

At the end of that year, Kenny and I travelled up to Coffs Harbour by car. Debbie took the time to drive me up to Gosford in the early morning to meet Kenny so it would shorten his drive.

Mum and Dad bought a villa in Toormina, which is closer to Coffs Harbour than Bonville was. This meant going "home" to a place I'd never seen before. It gave me a sad feeling knowing I wouldn't be going back to Bonville, where the family had had many good times over the past ten years.

The villa didn't have the space of the old house, so we went down to Boambee Reserve, which was close by. A creek ran through it, which made it ideal for swimming for those who couldn't handle or wanted a rest from the surf. There were a number of large shelters that people could book beforehand, so we didn't have to worry about the hot sun or sudden changes in the weather. There were coin-operated barbecues we frequently used.

It wasn't long into 1989 when the physiotherapy department at work offered me an electric wheelchair. They said it would conserve my body because I wouldn't have to walk as far as I had done previously. I found the wheelchair very handy in covering the broad expanse of Centre Industries.

People who would stop me and say something like, "That's good, Max. You've got an electric wheelchair," and I would reply, "It beats walkin'."

Other people showed their disappointment. They thought I had taken the easy way out. The fact was that I used the wheelchair only at work. Anyway, the people who were critical just didn't know the whole story.

I enjoyed working on the lock line, and our supervisor ran the bench like clockwork. Sometimes she was a pleasant person, and other times she had a sarcastic streak, which made it difficult for me to work with her. After twelve months or so I asked to be transferred to another workbench. When she found out I was leaving, she asked me if it was because of her. What could I say?

Our bus driver, John, who took us to work and back each day, had time for everyone who travelled with him and everyone else. We all thought a lot of John. It wasn't long after taking the run that he had a nickname for each one of us. Tony was Bones, Pip was Wombat, I was Squire, and so on. Even those who were on the bus for only a short time became a part of John's wit. We never saw John in a bad mood or saw him be impatient; he was always jovial. He saw each task as a challenge, smiling and joking all the way.

The unfortunate part concerning my friendship with John was that we didn't communicate as well as we should have. This wasn't the fault of either one of us. I would try not to talk to him while he was driving. I realised that he needed to concentrate on the road, so I didn't let my less-than-perfect speech distract him. When we were disembarking or boarding the bus, John was kept busy pushing people in wheelchairs up into the bus and clamping them down, so there wasn't much time for idle chatter. I've always maintained that John is an exceptional person.

Christmas 1989 came and went, with the new year bringing me another interest. I had been thinking about computers for a while. I wondered whether it would be beneficial to learn about them and whether they could make life easier for me. A small group of people from work enrolled in a computer course at a TAFE college for two hours one morning a week. This course was modified for people with disabilities, and it gave us a basic idea of what this modern tool could really do.

I was fascinated by the word processing module. Instead of writing something on the old typewriter and finishing with the page full of typing errors, it would come out of the printer as a clean-looking page. This is not to say I achieved anything like perfection at first, but the software had wonderful potential. I found it amazing that a group of words could be written and then changed and edited endlessly. I could make typing mistakes and have the instant facility to correct them.

I asked myself, "Why weren't computers around when I was in school?"

I went on to complete the course and then did Computer Studies 1, which was in a mainstream classroom. Someone sat beside me and wrote down notes for me. Unfortunately, this course was interrupted by circumstances beyond my control.

In May of that year, Kaye was visiting Jodie. She told me that Mum and Dad were coming to Sydney for a while because Dad had to spend some time in hospital. She said Kenny would pick me up either Saturday or Sunday, and we would go out to see them both. Mum was staying close by in hospital accommodations. Without losing sight of Dad's illness, it felt good to have them in Sydney. I realised after the third or fourth visit that Dad had cancer. This caused him to have a problem swallowing food. He had Venetian several times a day to clear his lungs and to prepare him for the operation that ultimately occurred.

While all that was happening, my rehabilitation councillor invited me to her office one day and gave me the opportunity to work in the mailroom in the administration section of the Spastic Centre. After outlining the job, she took me upstairs to meet Sue, the person who was in charge. When the introductions were over, they decided to grant me a two-week trial period. Then it was on to the mailroom, where I met two colleagues, Murray, who was also trying out for the job, and Betty, who had been carrying a box filled with mail since the early days of Centre Industries. Although I had known both of them for many years, I'd never had the pleasure of working with them.

At the end of the trial fortnight, my councillor asked me to come to her office again. She said, "Sue's been around to everyone to ask them if they were happy with your being the mail clerk, and everyone said they were." That gave me a great feeling. Then she said, "You've got the job." I was ecstatic. On the same day I was given the good news about the job, Dad had his operation. That night, when I arrived home, I had a telephone call from Mum, who said Dad was all right. Then I told her I had gotten the job.

The mailroom was an integral part of the Spastic Centre. It was where all the incoming mail was sorted. We sorted letters and other articles and put them in the various pigeonholes. On the rear of her wheelchair Betty had a box that had a large number of folders, so it was like a drawer in a filing cabinet. We transferred the items from the pigeonholes and placed them in the appropriate folders, which were labelled with people's names and their departments in alphabetical order. Then Betty went around the offices and departments, and people helped themselves to their own particular file.

When Betty was doing her rounds, we sorted out and helped distribute the internal mail. Most of it was in envelopes that had been used numerous times before, with the previous receiver's name crossed out. Occasionally courtesy wasn't practiced, and more than one name appeared on the envelope, which made it difficult to decipher. Then there was the bad handwriting. The internal mail came from all over the Spastic Centre. This was where my motorised wheelchair was very useful. I loaded up a small basket, held it on my lap, and drove around delivering mail.

The following weekend Kenny and I went to visit Dad. He wasn't a well man. How could he be? After all, he had just had a major operation. We felt sure things would improve, and they did for a while. Mum and Dad even went home. Two or three weeks later Dad was admitted to a private hospital in Coffs Harbours. Kenny and I were asked to go home because everyone thought that the end was near. We were there five or six days, and Dad remained stable. Kenny had to go home, and Kaye had to go to Sydney, so the family separated again.

Ten or so days later I was preparing to go to work when Kenny arrived at my door and said, "I've got some bad news for you." Before he had finished, I had guessed what he was going to say: that it was time to go back home for Dad's funeral. Although I offered to stay with Mum, she insisted that my life and job should come first.

Adrian, the chap I had replaced, returned. Fear of losing my job ran through my mind, but the decision was made that the three of us would work together in the mailroom. As time went on, Adrian and I became the best of friends. In fact, I began to admire him for the energy he put into his job and life generally. He was well-respected throughout the Spastic Centre. People had come to have tremendous trust in Adrian, and he was a thorough gentleman. It wouldn't be easy working up to Adrian standards, but I was keen to build a good reputation of my own.

Christmas came once again. Unfortunately, because I had had time away from the nursing home during the year, I could spend only a week with Mum. At a time when Mum needed company the most, it wasn't possible to stay with her because of some government regulation. The new year of 1991 came in smoothly, although, when I returned to the nursing home, it was difficult to settle down. I wanted so much to be with Mum.

Early in the new year, Sue invited the three of us mailroom workers around to her home for a barbecue. It was there that she told us of her resignation from the Spastic Centre. News of her leaving made us sad. Fortunately, we stayed in touch with her, as she gained employment just down the road from the Spastic Centre.

I think it was about a year later that Sue and her family had to move to Hong Kong because of her husband's work commitments. This wasn't the end of our friendship. Sue never forgot a birthday, although I have yet to find out the date of hers. I'm proud to say we still write to each other after seven years, and I hope to do so for many years to come. Adrian, Betty, and I worked harmoniously. Although Adrian went on a couple of experience terms, he was unable to find suitable outside employment.

It was a Sunday morning late in September 1991 that the Grand Final of the Rugby League was going to be played. As I was preparing for a day of watching football on television, Kenny arrived unexpectedly after staying overnight at a nearby caravan park. He had come to watch the football with me. We had waited since 1967, when Penrith came into the first division to win the Grand Final. Penrith had played Canberra the previous year on the big day, and they were beaten.

The day began with the President's Cup between Parramatta and Canterbury-Bankstown. After the Eels led by six points at half time, the Bulldogs went on to win in an exciting second half—twenty-two points to fourteen. The Reserve Grade match was between North Sydney and Canberra. This game was one-sided. The Bears were leading at the half time break, six to zero, and won the game at twelve points to six. Kenny and I were hoping that the Raiders would have the same destiny in the game.

It was time for the big match: Penrith against Canberra. After ten minutes the Captain, Royce Simmons, went over the try line for the Panthers and was converted, making the score six to zero. Kenny and I both breathed a sigh of relief. Soon after, the Raiders went over for their first try, but it was unconverted, which made the score six points to four. Then Canberra touched down for another try, making the halftime score ten points to six in favour of the Raiders. Kenny and I sweated through the half-time break. Quarter way through the second half, a tragedy happened, as Mark Geyer was sin binned for ten minutes. I think it was at that juncture that Kenny got up from his chair, feeling very disheartened.

The score was twelve points to six halfway through the final term when Canberra had a try disallowed. Then Brad Izzard of the Panthers scored another try, making it twelve points all. Then Penrith kicked a field goal seven minutes from full time, giving Penrith the lead by a point with four minutes of the game to go. The Panthers went over the try line once again, making the final score nineteen points to twelve. Penrith had won their first-ever first-grade Grand Final! Kenny became very emotional towards the end of the game. After twenty-four years, who could blame him? I think

Penrith's win meant more to Kenny than it did to me, but I was glad that we spent the day together.

About halfway through 1992 I was asked if I would take a course that the Spastic Centre was going to run. It involved basic data entry and bookkeeping. There was doubt in my mind because I thought I had the best job in the world, but I had the feeling that, if I didn't take this opportunity, I would be overlooked in the future. I could also use my newfound computer skills. At that stage the Spastic Centre had begun their decentralisation programme to follow government guidelines. This was also known as the transition period. It meant that, instead of having all the people with disabilities going to Allambie Heights to work and for other services, work and services would be available closer to their homes. It would also bring us more out in the community.

I wrote an article for our official opening that it gives a good overview of what we did during those ten weeks:

A New Way

It all began in August 1992 after the Spastic Centre of NSW purchased an Express Bookkeeping franchise and then decided to run a DEET-funded ten-week training course.

Apart from seven people with disabilities learning computer bookkeeping and seven in data entry, we were also taught about work practices, social skills, and small business management.

I remember the first day of the Data Entry and Bookkeeping course, or DEB, as it became known, when the introductions to the course were finished and everyone met each other, it was time for our first lesson in computer bookkeeping. I was nervous, not knowing much about keeping the financial records of a business, nor was I experienced using a computer. As time went on, I gained confidence. I had done a basic bookkeeping course at TAFE earlier the year to increase my knowledge.

On the second day, we met Julie Frankish (now Julie Gowen), who taught us work practices, social skills, and personal development. What we learnt from Julie during the ten weeks was both interesting and important.

Among the things we learnt from Julie, was the importance of having goals in life, both personally and in the workplace. We heard about time management and how important it is to plan one's day to get the maximum productivity from the time that is available.

Stress was another subject we discussed. Stress may have an effect on our relationship with other people. It can even be harmful to one's health.

By the end of DEB course, we all found Julie to be an excellent teacher who knew what she was talking about. She could communicate with us in a down-to-earth way but at the same time be professional. We came to know Julie as a lovely person.

Every Wednesday we had our lectures on small business management, made possible by Perry Tate and his men from MBA Systems. I think that one of the best things to come out of these sessions was our initial business plan. We put together this business plan under the capable guidance of Steve Sykes. The purpose of the business plan was, if DEB becomes our own business (which was the objective), to give us an idea of how to set our goals and what we have to do along the way to achieve them.

What I liked about doing the business plan was that, at the end of the course, we had it all down on paper. It was put into a book form so we could refer back to it.

We say a big thank you to the people at DEET for giving us a unique opportunity, making it possible for us to do the DEB course, and giving us the pleasure of working in Manly. Since we've been in Manly and out in the "real world", I think our quality of life has improved greatly.

One criticism I had of the course is that we weren't taught bookkeeping as such but only had a demonstration of the software. It was disappointing that there wasn't somewhere in the course a qualified teacher going through the basics of bookkeeping. There were other people in our little group who didn't have a bookkeeping background either.

We couldn't believe our good fortune when it was heard that our new business would be located in Manly, one of the northern beachside suburbs of Sydney.

We began working in Manly in late January 1993, after the break. Although I had seen the office before the renovations were done, as I walked into the office, I was impressed with how they had everything set up. At one end was a kitchenette with a brand-new refrigerator and microwave oven. The office was also well fitted out with a toilet for people with disabilities, which was just as well because the normal toilet was a flight of stairs away.

Working in the commercial area of Manly gave us a golden opportunity to buy fresh food for morning tea or lunch, do our banking, do some shopping, or just be in the sparkling atmosphere that this town had to offer. The government granted me a new electric wheelchair in late 1992, which couldn't have come at a better time, as it came in handy for use around Manly. Otherwise, I would have been stuck without "wheels".

Obviously we weren't there just to enjoy the sights and sounds of this town; there was a business to develop. The first job we had on the data entry side of the business was to enter the names and addresses from thousands of raffle tickets. This job came from the Spastic Centre. While it didn't exactly line our pockets with gold, it gave those of us who hadn't done data entry before valuable experience. There was a mystery surrounding the data entry programme. All the training that was done during the course went out the window because, when we started work in Manly, they changed the software, which meant more training. I was put on the data entry, rather than bookkeeping, which didn't worry me. It was disappointing to see some of my fellow workers not abide by the dress code that we decided upon during our course.

Frank went into Royal North Hospital again in 1992 for the third operation on his spine. I went to see him when he was recovering, and he seemed the same old Frank. The next time I saw him was one afternoon at work on my rounds delivering mail, when I entered the lift and saw Frank. They were taking him back up to the hostel. He was there for some respite care prior to going home. I really got a shock. Poor Frank: there he sat in the wheelchair with a wide strap around his waist. He had gone down so much that he was barely recognisable.

Memory doesn't recall the span of time, but Frank returned to his home, although there had been some doubt he ever would. I went up to visit him one weekend and found communication between us had become difficult. One thing that stands out in my mind that he said to me with a smile was "I got back home." I didn't continue seeing him, which left me with a bad feeling.

On May 17, 1993, I sat down at my desk after lunch, and our supervisor came up to me and said something like, "I got something to tell you. When I do, you can go away for a while. You can go outside. We've just heard from Pat Clark. Frank died this morning." Frank had been taken to Manly Hospital on the Friday before. I wish someone had told me, but who was to know the end was so close? Frank was my best friend, a real good mate for eighteen years. I will treasure forever the memory of his companionship. As you've read in this story, we shared many happy hours together, just talking about the things that we had in common, and there were many.

Christmas 1993 was fast approaching when a new manager was appointed to run our business. Marianne was an accountant; her skills brought valuable knowledge to our bookkeepers, and she knew something about data entry. Marianne arrived at a time when the atmosphere in the office was quite alarming. There were some people who choose not to follow office protocol. A group of people at one end of the room denigrated people working elsewhere in the office. There were days when I dreaded going to work. I've never had the ability to close myself out from what is going on around me. Sometimes I think I'm too sensitive for my own good. Another reason why there was discontent was that we had a supervisor who had little respect because he had a disability, and that made him fair game for some people.

I went home that year to a very hot summer. Bush fires were raging in many parts of the state. The situation became so bad around Mona Vale that I asked Mum to ring the nursing home to see that everyone and everything was all right. It was, thankfully. Mum talked me into staying an extra week, so I was late getting back to work, something that Marianne didn't let me forget for a few months after.

On the eve of my forty-sixth birthday, I had a visit from Frank's solicitor. He came to give me a gift that Frank lift in his will. Although I had received a copy of the will some months before, I was no less grateful for what a nice little nest egg Frank granted me.

Our first big data entry job came midway through 1994, when we gained work from Fisher & Pakel, the white goods manufacturer. We had to enter the information from warranty cards that came with the new appliances when people bought them. This was a good job that kept everyone busy.

When we started the DEB course, one failing we had was inferior equipment. We used ten or so second-hand computers that had been donated to the Spastic Centre. When we moved to Manly, they all were connected to a network. Right from day one, there were problems with the system. Sometimes we had to shut down all our computers because they would freeze; that is, we would be busily typing away when suddenly we couldn't key anymore. When that happened, all the computers had to be turned off for ten or fifteen minutes.

In early 1995 we had a lot of staff changes. Marianne disappeared mysteriously and another manager, Susan, came. She was a lovely person who knew a lot about computer programs. It was unfortunate that, just when she started, our data entry work began to dry up and remained just a trickle for months on end. They employed couple of accountants or bookkeepers to assist with the other half of the business.

Back in the old Centre Industries days, they would employ aides or attendants, as they are known these days. After having two attendant carers who were just all right and barely did their job, we welcomed Monica to our circle. Monica came from Centre Industries, where she had worked for about five years. She was well-trained and had a wealth of experience. She was an excellent worker and always did her best to meet everyone's needs. Above all that, Monica was and is a lovely person.

I went on a trip to Canberra with one of the better-known tour companies that specialised in travel for people with disabilities. The personal care was excellent, but when it came to following the itinerary, they left a lot to be desired. One young lady on the bus had to meet her relatives a couple of times, which threw the itinerary way off. The result was that we saw only about half of what was listed in the travel brochure. I wrote a letter to the company's manager to tell her of my discontent, and she replied by saying she was disappointed and would speak to the bus driver involved. The matter didn't go any farther.

In September 1995 Kenny and I went down to Canberra again. We stayed at a motel in Queanbeyan and travelled to the nation's capital each day. We didn't waste any time. On the first afternoon we drove up to Black Mountain to the Telstra Tower. From there we could see all over Canberra and far beyond. The Telstra Tower provides vital links in Australia's communications. Dramatically visible, the tower rises 195 metres and covers 2 hectares at its base. Arriving just before dusk, we viewed an amazing transformation. First we saw Canberra by day, with Lake Burley Griffin meandering through the city's centre and the various other buildings and landmarks. This gradually gave way to a brilliant array of colourful lights over a vast area as night crept in.

After returning from Black Mountain, we discovered a friendly watering hole, the Queanbeyan RSL Club, which served us well and was in walking distance from the motel. At the end of the day's activities, we enjoyed delicious hot meals and downed a few beers.

Beginning the next morning we tried to see or visit two or three venues a day, beginning with a very pleasant cruise around the lake. Other places we went were guided tours of the old historic Parliament House, the magnificent new Parliament House with its forecourt built from symbolic mosaic pavement, which tells the story of Aboriginal meeting places. The white marble in the Great Veranda was shining, and the Coat of Arms was just as beautiful. We went out on the rooftop beneath the stunning stainless steel flag mast that flies the Australian flag eighty-one metres above Parliament House.

We visited the Australian War Memorial, which is a national tribute to the 110,000 Australian men and women who have lost their lives in nine wars over the past 120 years. The National Science and Technology Centre was interesting, as visitors are provided with a remarkable experience designed to bring science and technology to life. The Royal Australian Mint, where all the coins are cast, was fascinating. The machinery they were operating reminded me of what was used in the old machine shop at Centre Industries. All too soon our trip ended. I came away from Canberra full of wonder and amazement about what it had to offer. More importantly, Kenny and I had a great time together.

Not far into 1997 we had some rumblings at work. There was talk about that DEB Services wasn't paying its way; that is, we weren't pulling in enough money to cover our expenses. Apart from not having much work, the rent in Manly must have been high.

Throughout the life of our business we were always encouraged to attend staff meetings to keep us informed about how things were going and to give us a chance to have our say. These meetings were held with no particular regularity. Sometimes we would meet as a whole group, and other times a number of us would meet as types of management committees, which were generally short-lived. Either way, when it was all said and done, it was only tokenism. A prime example of that was when they were deciding what to do to the save the business. Some people were asked—or in my case told—by the newly appointed marketing manager to be on the Salvage Committee. This committee was supposed to look at ways to make DEB Services viable. We looked at ways of cutting back on the transport costs, relocating to a cheaper site, or taking in other work that would pay better, like mail fulfilment.

In the end, the "Savage" Committee, as someone said, was an exercise in futility. If there had been a vote on the matter, I would bet that the vast majority of us would have liked to stay where we were, but the decision was made to split the business in two. The bookkeepers stayed in Manly and were joined with another work group that had been having a few problems with their host company but apparently could afford to pay their way.

The data entry people were shipped off to Sydney Employment Development Service (SEDS), which had become the employment arm of the Spastic Centre for people with disabilities. It was located at St. Lenards, an hour's drive from where most of us lived. We travelled each way by taxi. I really thought going towards the city in peak hour would cause long delays on the roads, but that didn't happen for the most part.

At SEDS we used two main rooms. One was our workroom, which was large and rectangular with a bench built around the walls. In one room we had our computers set up on it rather than having separate desks. The other room was used as an office for our new manager and her assistant, who doubled as our personal caregiver. We also used this room to have our morning tea and lunch. They weren't bad working conditions except when there was an overabundance of Mail fulfilment to do. There wasn't room to move.

Going out into the community at St. Lenards was difficult. Most shops and buildings had at least one step. Gone were the days when the people who used wheelchairs could go out and choose what they had for lunch. There were only two places I could get into in my wheelchair: the Medical Centre and the bank.

There was an occasion when we had a visit from many regional managers of the Spastic Centre. I was asked to write a sort story on the history of DEB Services. It does repeat some of what I've said earlier, but gives a more condensed, overall snapshot of the business.

DEB SERVICES IN A NUTSHELL

DEB Services began in January 1993 at a seaside suburb in the Northern Beach area of Sydney. We couldn't believe our good fortune when we heard that our new business would be located in Manly.

Working in the commercial area of Manly gave us a golden opportunity to escape into the "real world". We could go out to buy fresh food for our morning tea and lunch, do our banking or some shopping, or just take in the sparkling atmosphere that this town offers.

Obviously, though, we weren't there just to enjoy the sights and sounds of Manly. There was a new business to develop.

We had seven people trained in computer bookkeeping and another seven people trained to do data entry.

One of the first jobs we had on the data entry side of the business was to enter names and addresses from thousands of raffle tickets. This job came from the Spastic Centre. While it didn't exactly line our pockets with gold, it gave those of us who hadn't done data entry before valuable experience. Other clients we worked for in that first year were the AMP Society, Yves Saint Laurent (the cosmetic company), and Nicabates (the quit-smoking program).

The first really big job came in our second year of operation. It was with Fisher & Paykel. We entered information on the warranty cards from the customers who bought the company's "white goods". This job kept everyone busy for about fifteen months. We lost this job only because Fisher & Paykel changed over to bar codes.

Some of our more recent work has been for NRMA and Sydney Futures Exchange. With some of the newer work, we've diversified into fulfilment. This entails putting documents into envelopes and labelling them so they are ready to be posted.

Unfortunately, there's been a lot of downtime over the five or so years that DEB Service has been operating. Lack of productivity, of course, means not much money to remain functional.

Therefore, it was decided to relocate the data entry section to St. Leonards, where Sydney Employment Development Service (SEDS) could provide us with some office space for a nominal fee.

As much as we all loved working in Manly and would miss it terribly, it was time to think of the business and our future. The move was beneficial for us within the first few weeks. As well as keeping Pharmaceutical Marketing and Sydney Futures, we have picked up several other jobs in both data entry and fulfilment packaging.

We hope that we will return to the Northern Beaches within twelve to eighteen months—maybe not Manly but somewhere in the Northern Beaches area.

In May 1997 I asked Kenny to accompany me to the Witsunday Islands just off the Queensland coast. After deciding on an island on which to stay, Kenny made all the booking arrangements for a seven-day holiday on South Mole Island. We began our journey by driving to Sydney Airport on a Wednesday afternoon and staying at the Airport Hilton Hotel overnight. Around midmorning the next day, we boarded the aeroplane to Hamilton Island, where we made a brief stop-over before catching a launch over to South Mole Island. We arrived at the jetty and were greeted by some friendly people who work at the resort. Then we boarded a golf buggy and were driven to a central location to be given a rundown on where the facilities were and some of the day-to-day activities, both organized and independent, on South Mole.

The first evening we enjoyed a bush barbecue with many kinds Australian foods on the menu. I had my first taste of kangaroo meat. It tasted like any other meat to me. Other theme nights were a South Pacific night with seafood and island-style singing and dancing, and a night on which the entertainment staff put on a stage show. They sang and danced the musical, *Grease*. I thought it was very professionally done.

One evening Kenny went on a sunset hike while I sat poolside enjoying a beer or two. While Kenny was gone, the weather changed. One of the entertainment men suggested I should move indoors, so when Kenny returned, I was nowhere to be seen. After searching for me for some time, he entered the bar area and saw me sitting at the bar. The two wonderful photographs that Kenny took of the sun going down will be treasured for many years. They really are magnificent.

By day we involved ourselves in some of the activities. Kenny got a catamaran, and after donning life jackets, we sailed out some distance from the shore. It was a calm day, which made the sailing slow. This probably was a blessing in disguise because, if we had picked up any speed, I don't think I could have kept my balance, even though I was sitting on the deck and hanging on to a guide wire. After our sailing adventure, I waded at the water's edge doing my old hands-and-knees trick.

One of the main reasons I wanted to go to the Witsundays was to see the Great Barrier Reef. The day came when we caught a Fantasea Cruise to see this world-renowned sight. The trip took two hours. When we reached the pontoon, we climbed down into a small, glass-bottomed submarine to view many breeds and colours of fish. I was a bit disappointed in the colour of the coral, but someone said it was because of the cloudy day. Kenny did some snorkelling in a controlled area. If I had the chance to go to the reef again, I would jump at it, but on sunny day.

A couple of days before we left South Mole, we did a tour of Hamilton Island. By hiring a golf buggy, we were able to explore the island extensively. It was like a small city with its high-rise buildings. The swimming pools were plentiful, and some of them covered a wide area. There was so much greenery around the place that it looked like it just had been planted and gave the landscaped gardens an artificial appearance. After a rushed lunch, we boarded a ferry again to have a look at Whitehaven Beach. This is one of the most outstanding and unique sandscapes in Australia. Situated on the eastern, uninhabited side of Whitsunday Island, it is a spectacular and pristine environment with its powdery white sand and crystal clear water. A few days before it was time to leave South Mole Island, people started asking me when Kenny and I were going home. I said with a smile, "We're not!"

The staff on South Mole Island were wonderful. Wherever we went and whatever we did, they were there to lend a hand. Their friendliness, professionalism, and unobtrusiveness made our stay most enjoyable. As Kenny often said, "It's very laid back."

Unlike Hamilton Island, South Mole had a natural setting. The buildings were scattered and low-rise. They nestled amongst the island's flora. I took great delight in sitting on the front patio, where the birds landed on my arms and legs and even on my head. One bird helped itself to a taste of my top lip.

There was one misgiving concerning our room. When we booked the holiday, we asked for a room to suit a person with a disability. The bathroom wasn't in any way fitted out to assist me. The shower was above a bath, and I had to climb over the side of the bath at shower time. I don't know what would have happened if I had been confined to the wheelchair. However, the room was spacious, making it easy manoeuver around, and it had a ramp leading up to the back door. After we returned from South Mole, I wrote a letter to the island's management, pointing out the problems with the bathroom. I received a letter back that thanked me for bringing their attention to my difficulties.

One evening around April 1997, soon after arriving home from work, I had a visit from a house manager who was employed by the Spastic Centre. The house manager asked me whether I was interested sharing a home in Mona Vale with Jeff. I had known Jeff ever since I started working at Centre Industries, and his wife Cathy and I had come to know each other when she and Jeff began travelling on our work bus. Cathy and Jeff had gone on an overseas trip earlier that year. Unfortunately, Cathy died on the aeroplane just before it touched down in Sydney. Kenny came down one weekend, and we went to visit the house. We stayed for four hours talking to Jeff and one of his caregivers. They were kind enough to give us lunch.

Three or four months later I made the big move. Of course, I was apprehensive about living in a house with one other person with a disability and not having the security of staff on hand twenty-four hours a day. My family was supportive of the change, which was surprising. When I first moved in, Jeff was protective of the house, and that was completely understandable. After all, it was Jeff's and Cathy's home for seven or eight years. In some ways, I think Jeff's privacy must have been invaded, not only by me but also the people from Home Care, who were total strangers.

Jeff and Cathy had always been looked after by staff from the Spastic Centre, who did their personal care and general running of the house. When I moved in, there wasn't enough funding for both Jeff and me (something I couldn't understand), so people from Home Care of NSW were brought in to take care of my daily needs. Having two caregivers from two organizations became chaotic, particularly when they were cooking dinner. I mean, even the fringe had to be divided into two sections, and we each had to buy our own food. We were using Jeff's appliances and utensils, such as the fridge, the washing machine, pots and pans, crockery, and cutlery.

Jeff and I each had a bedroom and a lounge room. The only problem was that I had to walk from my lounge room through Jeff's lounge room to get to my bedroom. It made me feel uncomfortable in the beginning. As time went on, we managed to tolerate and then enjoy each other's company, not that there was ever any great tension between us. Things became much more civilized when the Spastic Centre took over my care the next February.

One of the better things to come out of having the Home Care Service for those few months was that I met a lovely lady. Robyn and I had an instant rapport. She was an excellent worker and did her utmost to make me feel at home in my new environment. Fortunately, Robyn decided to seek employment by the Spastic Centre to enable her to continue working at our house.

Living with Jeff didn't present many problems. The house was big enough so we didn't get in each other's way. The only time we really came together was at the dinner table, where there was always fun and laughter. Each Saturday we ate breakfast and then helped to write a shopping list with our caregiver, Ken. Then we all went down to Warriewood Square in Jeff's van. After we got there, Jeff and I left Ken to do the shopping while we roamed some of the other stores. Occasionally, on a Friday evening when Ken was working, we went out for dinner. Sometimes we went to The Mona Vale RSL, and other times we went somewhere like a pizza place.

In March 1998 Kenny and I celebrated our fiftieth birthdays. Kenny invited me up to his place for a few days. The night before our big day, Kenny and I were picked up in a stretch car and drank a glass of champagne while being driven to a restaurant in Terrigal, a beachside town on the Central Coast. We were met by Larraine, Nicole, Dwayne, and some of their friends. We had lovely evening. Everyone went out of their way to help us to celebrate reaching the half-century mark.

There was a new entertainment centre in Sydney, and I asked Kenny whether he would like to spend part of our birthday there. Star City Casino opened in late 1997 with 200 gaming tables and 1,500 poker machines, catering to a diverse range of people. It also includes a 480-room hotel, two theatres, and seven major restaurants. I tried my hand with a poker machine, but the gambling devil wasn't kind to me, even on my birthday. At least I scored a "Star City" cap from our coach driver. I had a great birthday, as I'm sure Kenny did, particularly since it was spread over a few days.

It must have been April or May when my community worker, Judy, came to see me. She said that the Department of Housing was building a block of home units in Brookvale, and my name appeared on the waiting list. This was strange because, when I moved in with Jeff, my name was to be taken off the list. A few days later Judy and I went to have a look at the unit that had been allocated to me.

When we first saw the unit, it wasn't finished. It was at a lock-up stage, basically. It was one of twenty-three residences, right at the front of the complex. We walked in to find a large bathroom and laundry combined, a generously sized bedroom, a small kitchen, and a spacious lounge and dining area. Although it was difficult to see just how big the rooms were with building materials and tools stored throughout the place, I decided there and then I wanted to make it my home. Surprisingly again, the family was on my side.

The next thing I had to do was to tell Jeff, Ken, and Robyn. I let the cat out of the bag somewhat to Robyn because I asked her one evening, "Does your home care cover Brookvale?"

Robyn sensed there was something happening. A short time later that night, she asked me, "Max, what is going on?" Even though I told her to forget about it, I eventually told her. Although I'd mentioned it to Jeff a couple of weeks earlier—mainly because of where he worked, and I didn't want him to hear anything before I told him—one Tuesday evening over I took the opportunity to tell Jeff and Ken when the three of us were together. At the time I believed Ken was upset that I was moving on, but he understood my position.

One Sunday morning I woke up feeling unwell, and as the day went on, my illness worsened. I had to ask our caregiver to take me to the local medical centre. It wasn't long after having a chest x-ray that I was admitted to Mona Vale Hospital suffering from pneumonia. Robyn came to see me that afternoon. She was genuinely concerned for me and asked whether I needed anything. Kenny came the next morning and spent most of the day with me. Mum travelled to Kenny's place that Monday, and both came to the hospital on the Tuesday for the day. My stint in hospital lasted for five days, during which I wasn't confined to bed at all. In fact, they encouraged to keep walking around to help to clear my chest. Ken visited me in hospital several times.

Robyn was most helpful. She dropped in often, even coming back to the hospital four and five times one particularly day. In the weeks and months that followed, in our quieter moments together and on more than one occasion, I had the chance to say to her, "You're wonderful, Robyn."

I was released from hospital on Friday and began a six-week recovery period before returning to work. Mum and Kenny came that weekend, and I was able to take them to see the new unit, although Kenny had seen it once before.

On September 16, 1998, I moved to Brookvale. Mum, Kenny, and Larraine helped with the move. We organised a small removalist van to take my furniture to my new unit. Mum had the task of unpacking everything, while Larraine helped me with the layout of the furniture in the bedroom.

Kenny had put up a couple of selves in my room at the nursing home that I hadn't used at the house. He had the idea of screwing them to the wall to hold my small cassette player and speakers. It worked out perfectly. With his trusty electric drill he also screwed many hooks into the masonry to hang pictures, photographs, and other items on. Kenny was drilling holes for two or three months before we got things right. He still says that, if he took all the screws out of wall, the place would fall down.

Late that day the new refrigerator and washing machine arrived. This really brought it home to me that the move was a good one and had permanence. Mum had to stay with me for the six weeks because there were two main problems. One was that I didn't have a hands-free telephone, which is much easier for me to use than a normal one. All it takes is a press of a button, rather than having to lift the receiver. The other problem was that, when the hot water system was installed, they put a governor on the hot water to guard against people with a disability scalding themselves—not that it was such a good regulator. The heat of the water fluctuated constantly. The Home Care staff was always going to help me with my shower, so my ability to control the heat of the water didn't matter. We had to write a letter to the Department of Housing stating that I wouldn't be using the hot water by myself. A similar letter had to be sent by my community support worker at the Spastic Centre.

My unit is just at the rear of Warringah Mall, which is the prime shopping centre complex on the Pittwater Peninsular. The mall was undergoing a major upgrade, and it was interesting to see the gradual transformation. Most of the shops were rebuilt, and many new retailers opened for the first time. Over the few years since I've been here, many businesses have come and gone. A lot of smaller shops that duplicate products and services make the composition fierce.

Not long after I returned to work, there were moves afoot to relocate back to the Northern Beaches area. They had a few places in mind, two of which were in Brookvale. One was just around the corner from my unit. One rostered day off, some other people and I were asked to have a look at the site. When we saw it, I said, "This is the place." However, my approval was purely selfish because, if the building were accepted as our new workplace, it would mean no more catching taxis to work; I could drive there in my electric wheelchair.

To get to and from work each day, I had to cross Old Pittwater Road, which can be busy, particularly in peak periods. What made it worse was that the new workplace was on a bend in the road, which made it dangerous to cross at this spot. With the help of a friend, we found it would be safer if I crossed the road the end of my street. From there I went up a side street about fifty metres, crossed over, came down the other side, and rounded a corner to the driveway of the industrial estate.

This industrial estate was one of many in Brookvale. Our unit had a large warehouse at one end and a two-storey office block. We were joined by the group of people who took our place in Manly. They were able to take full advantage of the warehouse space. Those of us who worked on computers were reunited with the bookkeepers we left in Manly.

We occupied the downstairs office area. The upper level was accessed by a staircase, so it was out of reach for most people with a disability. As time went on, we found the conditions we were working under were uncomfortable to say the least. There were two toilets at one side of the office with people coming in and out all day. Often a conversation began between an office worker with whoever came in, and everyone lost concentration. One person took it upon herself to watch the toilet doors and announce to the world who was in the toilet. This caught on, and other people started to do it.

We had a kitchenette and a dining table in one corner of the warehouse. One day I complained about the flies around the lunch table and was told that nothing could be done about it.

One thing that went against DEB Services, I think, was all of the managers—or facilitators, as they liked to be called—that were in charge. We had three in Manly, not including the first man, who had his own business to run, and one in St. Leonards, who was a schoolteacher by profession. Sometimes I felt more like one of her pupils than an employee. There were a couple of young facilitators in charge when we started in Brookvale. I don't think their tender years did us or our business any favours. In one period, people had to beg for attendant care. More than once I had a disabled colleague help me with lunch. Once we were told that no person with a disability was allowed to assist people with their meals, but this was forgotten about the very next day. No one at lower management level has had a chance to build any real rapport with the business or its employees.

As the years went by, the situation in the office worsened. The data entry work dried up completely. The bookkeepers went back to the accounts section at the Spastic Centre. Some of the computers were taken away, and the rest were moved to one side of the office. They placed a workbench in the centre on which to do mail fulfilment or whatever other job that came along. This increased the noise level. Occasionally I helped out on the table or went out into the warehouse to lend a hand. Of course, I couldn't do a lot of the jobs. This gave a welcome break from doing my own work on my computer or just sitting there and watching other people work. This was all right until some real computer work came along.

Glenn, our bookkeeping supervisor, returned to Brookvale and asked to set a timesheet job for all the Spastic Centre work sites that employ the people with disabilities. Eventually I was able help enter the data for those timesheets. I enjoyed doing this job, but there wasn't enough work to keep me going all day every day. Living close to work gave me the advantage of going home before knock-off time when there wasn't any work for me. I'd always ask permission first, of course.

The last five years have been the happiest of my life. I've enjoyed living on my own, and my life has been enriched. I believe I'm living life at its full potential in light of my disability. I'm very proud of my little unit. It gives me a great feeling when people come in to my home and say how nice it looks and how tidy it is. I run a tight ship in that regard. Untidiness or not having things clean just isn't good enough for me. Fortunately, I have a wonderful lady from Home Care who does my housework and shopping. Trish is one of these people who never worries about how big the workload is or how long it takes.

I feel a part of the community and am proud to be part of it. I haven't worked on a Friday for a few years, preferring to have that day to myself and choosing not to have any real lunch. I have a cup of coffee as soon as I get there, and a milkshake just before coming home. I often spend time at the mall shopping or just looking. Sometimes temptation gets its way, and I buy something that, perhaps, I could do without. By way of change sometimes I might catch a wheelchair-accessible bus and travel up to Warriewood Shopping Centre, formerly known as Warriewood Square. I've always liked this shopping centre, mainly for its size. Since now I'm always in the electric wheelchair, it isn't a problem covering large areas. My love affair with Manly continues. I still enjoy its atmosphere and charm. It's only a ten-minute run on the bus from the mall to Manly Wharf.

Since I left the house in Mona Vale, Jeff, Robyn, Ken, and I have stayed in contact. We go out to one of the nearby clubs. Although Jeff has moved away from the area, it doesn't prevent him from catching a taxi and having a good evening with us. The friendship between Jeff and me goes back a long way and will remain for many years to come.

Ken keeps himself busy. Apart from his work, he volunteers much of his time to charity. However, he can always find a moment to visit people, regardless of the shortage of time. Ken drops in to see me most Tuesday afternoons on the way to work, even though it may be only a minute or two. I have told him on several occasions just how proud I am of our friendship. Ken is one in a million.

I mentioned earlier how wonderful Robyn has been to me. She is a rare person. No one will ever know how much she inspired me. We don't see much of each other these days, but the moments I had with Robyn are cherished memories. The only thing I found disappointing about my relationship with Robyn is that I couldn't full in love with her.

Two or three times a year I have lunch with Monica. We usually go to the Dee Why RSL Club with a few people from work. Monica, too, is an extraordinary person with time and compassion for everyone who comes into her life. I marvel at her warmth and sincerity.

Around September or October of 2002, thoughts of retiring began to enter my mind. In March 2003 I would turn fifty-five, so the decision was logical and not difficult to make.

Since retiring, I go once or twice a month on a day trip with Disabled Alternative Road Travel Service (DARTS). The purpose of this organisation is to arrange and provide modified vans for people who use a wheelchair. They have outings almost every day that go all over Sydney and beyond. Since I've been going out with DARTS, they have taken me up to the Central Coast, down to the Illawarra Area, out to the Blue Mountains, and all over the metropolitan area. I've been to venues like shopping centres, theatres, restaurants, sporting clubs, and RSL clubs. They know how to throw a midyear or an end-of-year party. The organisation is always superb. DARTS trains their drivers and volunteer helpers professionally, so outings run smoothly. Their office administration is also professional.

It's been fifteen months since I retired, and looking back over that period, I can say that retiring was the right decision. I wake each morning eager to take part in whatever has to be done or, much more often, whatever I choose to do.

At the end of 1999 I gave copies of this document to my family and some friends. At that stage it was forty-three pages long and should have had the word "draft" stamped all over it because it hadn't been proofread. Unfortunately, I didn't get as much feedback as I would have liked. A couple of comments I received were that I didn't put enough feeling or emotion into my story and that I needed to "give the reader a little more insight into the people you have been involved with—make them more real (alive)."

I feel have put as much of myself into writing this book; whether that is enough I will leave to others to judge.